# Table of contents

| | |
|---|---|
| **The Ketogenic Lifestyle** | **1** |
| Introduction to the Ketogenic Lifestyle | 1 |
| Benefits of the Ketogenic Diet | 2 |
| Adapting Greek Cuisine for the Ketogenic Diet | 4 |
| **Greek Breakfasts** | **6** |
| Spinach and Feta Omelette | 7 |
| Greek Yogurt Parfait with Berries and Nuts | 8 |
| Keto Spanakopita Quiche | 9 |
| Keto Greek Breakfast Casserole | 10 |
| **Keto Appetizers** | **11** |
| Greek Lemon and Garlic Chicken Skewers | 12 |
| Low-Carb Greek Salad Skewers | 13 |
| Keto Tzatziki Dip with Veggie Sticks | 14 |
| Greek Zucchini Balls (Kolokithokeftedes) | 15 |
| **Soups and Salads** | **17** |
| Creamy Keto Avgolemono Soup | 18 |
| Greek Cucumber Salad with Feta and Olives | 19 |
| Keto Greek Salad with Grilled Chicken | 20 |
| Low-Carb Stuffed Pepper Soup | 22 |
| **Mains and Sides** | **23** |
| Lemon and Herb Grilled Chicken Souvlaki | 24 |
| Keto Moussaka with Eggplant | 26 |
| Greek Style Stuffed Bell Peppers | 28 |
| Keto Greek Stuffed Chicken Breast | 30 |
| **Greek Desserts** | **32** |
| Keto Baklava Cheesecake Bars | 33 |
| Greek Yogurt Panna Cotta with Berry Sauce | 35 |
| Low-Carb Loukoumades (Greek Donuts) | 37 |
| Keto Galaktoboureko (Custard Pie) | 39 |
| **Cuisine Fusion (Greek and Other Cuisines)** | **41** |
| Mediterranean Keto Buddha Bowl | 42 |
| Greek-inspired Keto Pizza | 44 |
| Keto Greek Nachos with Lamb | 46 |
| Greek-style Cauliflower Tabbouleh | 48 |
| **Special Occasions and Entertaining** | **50** |
| Keto Moussaka Sliders | 51 |
| Lemon and Garlic Shrimp Skewers | 53 |
| Low-Carb Spanakopita Bites | 54 |
| Greek-style Mini Meatballs with Tzatziki Sauce | 56 |
| **Outro: Embracing the Ketogenic Lifestyle** | **58** |

# The Ketogenic Lifestyle

## Introduction to the Ketogenic Lifestyle

Welcome to the exciting world of the ketogenic lifestyle, where we embark on a journey of transforming traditional Greek cuisine into delicious, low-carb, and keto-friendly dishes. In this chapter, we will delve into the fundamentals of the ketogenic diet, explore its numerous benefits, and discover how we can adapt the rich and vibrant flavors of Greek cuisine to suit this unique way of eating.

The ketogenic lifestyle has gained immense popularity in recent years, not only for its effectiveness in weight loss but also for its potential health benefits. By following a low-carb, high-fat diet, our bodies enter a state of ketosis, where they rely on fat for fuel rather than glucose. This metabolic shift can lead to increased energy levels, mental clarity, and improved overall well-being.

Within the pages of this book, you will find a collection of mouthwatering recipes that showcase the beauty and diversity of Greek cuisine while adhering to the principles of the ketogenic diet. From breakfasts that will kickstart your day to appetizers that will impress your guests, and from satisfying main courses to indulgent desserts, we have curated a selection of dishes that will make your taste buds dance with joy.

But this journey is about more than just transforming recipes. It's about embracing the ingredients, techniques, and traditions that make Greek cuisine so unique, while adapting them to align with our keto goals. By exploring the flavors of Greece through a ketogenic lens, we can enjoy the tastes we love while nourishing our bodies with wholesome, low-carb ingredients.

Join me as we embark on this culinary adventure, paying homage to the vibrant world of Greek cuisine while embracing the transformative power of the ketogenic lifestyle. Let the flavors of the Mediterranean and the principles of keto guide us towards a healthier, more vibrant life.

So grab your apron, sharpen your knives, and get ready to savor the best of both worlds – the tantalizing taste of Greek cuisine and the benefits of a ketogenic lifestyle. Together, we will explore the vibrant flavors and nourishing ingredients that will revolutionize your perception of Greek food, leaving you feeling energized, satisfied, and excited about your culinary endeavors.

Are you ready to embark on this delectable journey? Let's dive in!

## Benefits of the Ketogenic Diet

The ketogenic diet has garnered significant attention in recent years, and for good reason. Beyond its reputation for weight loss, this low-carb, high-fat lifestyle offers a multitude of benefits that can positively impact both our physical and mental well-being. In this segment, we will explore some of the key advantages of adopting the ketogenic diet and how it can transform your health.

1. Improved Weight Management: One of the most well-known benefits of the ketogenic diet is its ability to support weight loss and weight management. By reducing carbohydrate intake and focusing on healthy fats and moderate protein, the body shifts from glucose to fat metabolism. This metabolic state, known as ketosis, promotes the burning of stored fat for energy, leading to steady and sustainable weight loss over time.

2. Enhanced Mental Clarity and Focus: Many individuals have reported experiencing improved mental clarity, focus, and cognitive function while following a ketogenic diet. By providing a stable source of energy to the brain through ketones, rather than the fluctuating glucose levels associated with a high-carb diet, the ketogenic lifestyle can help support clear thinking, increased productivity, and improved memory.

3. Increased Energy Levels: Say goodbye to those mid-afternoon energy crashes! The ketogenic diet can provide a steady and sustained energy supply throughout the day. By tapping into our body's fat stores for fuel, rather than relying on the quick but short-lived energy derived from carbohydrates, we can experience improved endurance, increased stamina, and reduced feelings of fatigue.

4. Balanced Blood Sugar Levels: For those struggling with insulin resistance or diabetes, the ketogenic diet offers a promising solution. By limiting carbohydrate intake, the ketogenic lifestyle helps regulate blood sugar levels and can lead to improved insulin sensitivity. This can have significant long-term benefits, including better blood sugar control, reduced risk of complications, and improved overall metabolic health.

5. Reduced Inflammation: Chronic inflammation has been linked to various health issues, including heart disease, autoimmune conditions, and certain types of cancer. The ketogenic diet has shown potential in reducing inflammation by limiting the intake of inflammatory foods, such as sugar and processed carbohydrates, and promoting the consumption of anti-inflammatory fats and nutrient-dense whole foods.

6. Appetite Regulation and Reduced Cravings: When following a ketogenic diet, the high intake of healthy fats and moderate protein helps promote satiety, effectively curbing cravings and reducing excessive hunger. This can be a significant advantage for those looking to maintain a caloric deficit for weight loss or those striving to make healthier food choices.

By embracing the ketogenic lifestyle and adapting Greek cuisine to align with its principles, we unlock a world of flavors and health benefits that go hand-in-hand. In the coming chapters, we will explore how we can infuse traditional Greek dishes with keto-friendly ingredients, maintaining the essence of the Mediterranean diet while reaping the rewards of a low-carb, high-fat lifestyle. Get ready to experience the transformative power of the ketogenic diet, Greek style!

## Adapting Greek Cuisine for the Ketogenic Diet

Greek cuisine is renowned for its vibrant flavors, fresh ingredients, and wholesome dishes. From the iconic moussaka to the tangy tzatziki and hearty souvlaki, Greek food has a special place in our hearts and palates. In this segment, we will explore the art of adapting Greek cuisine to adhere to the principles of the ketogenic diet while preserving the essence and authenticity of these beloved dishes.

The key to successfully adapting Greek cuisine for the ketogenic lifestyle lies in making thoughtful ingredient substitutions and modifications. By swapping out high-carb ingredients with low-carb alternatives and increasing the use of healthy fats, we can transform traditional Greek recipes into keto-friendly creations without compromising on taste or enjoyment.

Let's take a look at some common ingredients and techniques used in Greek cooking and explore how we can adapt them for a ketogenic twist:

1. Replacing Carbohydrate-rich Ingredients: Traditional Greek dishes often include ingredients like potatoes, grains, and flours, which can be high in carbohydrates. To create keto-friendly versions of these dishes, we can substitute potatoes with low-carb alternatives like cauliflower or turnips, use almond or coconut flour instead of wheat flour, and replace grains with nutrient-dense options such as quinoa or cauliflower rice.

2. Embracing Healthy Fats: Greek cuisine already incorporates healthy fats in the form of olive oil, which is a staple of the Mediterranean diet. On a ketogenic diet, we can further emphasize the use of healthy fats like avocado oil, coconut oil, and ghee in our cooking. These fats not only provide a rich flavor but also help us reach our desired macronutrient ratio for ketosis.

3. Incorporating High-quality Proteins: Greek cuisine is known for its delicious grilled meats, seafood, and dairy products. When adapting recipes for the ketogenic diet, we can prioritize high-quality, lean proteins like chicken, lamb, and fish, which are excellent sources of essential nutrients. Additionally, we can incorporate Greek yogurt and feta cheese, which provide a creamy and tangy element to many dishes.

4. Enhancing Flavor with Herbs and Spices: Greek cuisine is celebrated for its aromatic herbs and spices, which add depth and complexity to dishes. We can continue to use herbs like oregano, basil, and dill, along with spices such as cinnamon and nutmeg, to elevate the flavors of our keto-friendly creations. These seasonings not only enhance taste but also offer various health benefits, such as antioxidant and anti-inflammatory properties.

By embracing these adaptations and understanding the art of balancing flavors, we can transform traditional Greek dishes into mouthwatering, ketogenic-friendly creations that nourish our bodies and tantalize our taste buds. Throughout this book, we will navigate the intricate world of Greek cuisine, exploring the synergy between delicious flavors and the ketogenic lifestyle.

So, let's dive into the following chapters, where we will embark on a culinary journey through Greek breakfasts, tantalizing appetizers, hearty soups and salads, satisfying mains and sides, decadent desserts, innovative cuisine fusion, and special occasion recipes. Together, let's unlock the immense potential of Greek cuisine in the context of the ketogenic lifestyle and redefine how we approach a low-carb, high-fat way of eating. Get ready to experience the best of both worlds as we embark on this delicious adventure!

## Greek Breakfasts

Καλημέρα (Kalimera)! Good morning! In this chapter, we will dive into the delightful world of Greek breakfasts and discover how to infuse them with keto-friendly ingredients. Greek breakfasts are a celebration of fresh flavors, wholesome ingredients, and a time to gather and enjoy a leisurely meal with loved ones. And now, we have the opportunity to adapt these morning delights to embrace the ketogenic lifestyle.

Breakfast is often considered the most important meal of the day, and with Greek culture deeply rooted in the Mediterranean diet, it comes as no surprise that Greek breakfasts feature an array of nutritious and delicious ingredients. From eggs and feta cheese to yogurt and vibrant Mediterranean vegetables, Greek breakfasts have a little something for everyone.

By utilizing the principles of the ketogenic diet, we can enhance the nutritional profile of these traditional Greek breakfasts while maintaining their delightful flavors. Whether you're looking for a quick and easy meal to start your day or a leisurely brunch to savor, the Greek breakfast recipes in this chapter will inspire you to kick-start your mornings with a keto twist.

Greek breakfasts are known for their simple yet elegant combinations, showcasing the natural flavors of the ingredients. In this chapter, we will explore a variety of delicious and satisfying keto Greek breakfast recipes. From hearty omelettes filled with savory fillings to parfaits bursting with the freshness of berries and nuts, these recipes will energize you for the day ahead while keeping your macros in check.

So, Greek food enthusiasts and keto devotees, get ready to indulge in a symphony of flavors as we embark on this journey through Greek breakfasts with a ketogenic twist. Brimming with nutrient-dense ingredients, these recipes will fuel your body, nourish your soul, and transport you to the sunny shores of Greece with every bite.

Join me in discovering the art of creating Greek breakfasts that are not only delicious but also support your ketogenic lifestyle goals. From the scent of warm oregano to the tang of creamy Greek yogurt, let's celebrate the enticing flavors of Greece in the comfort of our own kitchens.

Prepare to rise and shine with the delectable keto Greek breakfast recipes that await you in the next section. From fluffy omelettes to refreshing yogurt parfaits, we're about to transform your mornings into a delightful Mediterranean keto experience. Let's begin this culinary adventure and taste the joy of Greek breakfasts, keto-style!

## Spinach and Feta Omelette

Start your day with a burst of Mediterranean flavors by treating yourself to a delightful Spinach and Feta Omelette. This protein-packed keto Greek breakfast combines the earthy flavors of fresh spinach with the creamy tang of feta cheese, creating a harmonious balance that will leave you satisfied and energized.

Ingredients:
- 3 large eggs
- 1 tablespoon olive oil
- 1 cup fresh spinach, roughly chopped
- 1/4 cup crumbled feta cheese
- Salt and pepper, to taste

Instructions:
1. Crack the eggs into a mixing bowl and whisk them until well combined. Season with a pinch of salt and pepper.
2. Heat the olive oil in a non-stick frying pan over medium heat.
3. Add the chopped spinach to the pan and sauté for 1-2 minutes until wilted.
4. Pour the whisked eggs into the pan, allowing them to coat the spinach evenly.
5. Sprinkle the crumbled feta cheese on top of the omelette mixture.
6. Cook for 2-3 minutes, or until the bottom is set and lightly golden.
7. Using a spatula, carefully fold one side of the omelette over the other, creating a half-moon shape.
8. Continue cooking for another minute until the feta cheese starts to melt.
9. Slide the omelette onto a plate and garnish with additional crumbled feta, if desired.
10. Serve hot and enjoy your deliciously keto-friendly Spinach and Feta Omelette.

This savory and satisfying omelette is not only a delicious way to start your day but also a wonderful source of essential nutrients. Spinach provides a rich source of vitamins and minerals, while feta cheese adds a generous dose of calcium and protein. Combined with the healthy fats in eggs and olive oil, this breakfast will keep you feeling full and nourished for hours.

So, whether you're enjoying a leisurely morning or need a quick and nutritious breakfast on the go, this Spinach and Feta Omelette will become a go-to keto Greek dish to fuel your day. Prepare to savor the flavors of Greece while embracing the benefits of the ketogenic lifestyle with each delightful bite. Yasou, and enjoy!

## Greek Yogurt Parfait with Berries and Nuts

Indulge in a luscious and satisfying Greek Yogurt Parfait with Berries and Nuts to elevate your breakfast to a whole new level of deliciousness. This keto Greek breakfast offers a delightful combination of creamy Greek yogurt, vibrant berries, and crunchy nuts, creating a symphony of flavors and textures that will leave your taste buds begging for more.

Ingredients:
- 1 cup plain Greek yogurt
- 1 tablespoon of your preferred keto sweetener (optional)
- 1/4 cup mixed berries (such as blueberries, raspberries, or strawberries)
- 2 tablespoons chopped nuts (such as almonds, walnuts, or pistachios)
- A drizzle of sugar-free honey or a sprinkle of cinnamon (optional)

Instructions:
1. In a bowl, combine the plain Greek yogurt and sweetener (if desired), and mix well until smooth and creamy.
2. In a glass or a breakfast bowl, layer half of the Greek yogurt mixture.
3. Add a layer of mixed berries on top of the yogurt, distributing them evenly.
4. Sprinkle a tablespoon of chopped nuts over the berries.
5. Repeat the layers by adding the remaining Greek yogurt, followed by another layer of mixed berries.
6. Finish the parfait by sprinkling the remaining chopped nuts on top.
7. If desired, drizzle a small amount of sugar-free honey or sprinkle a pinch of cinnamon over the parfait for added flavor.
8. Serve immediately and enjoy the tantalizing combination of creamy Greek yogurt, juicy berries, and crunchy nuts.

This Greek Yogurt Parfait not only satisfies your taste buds but also offers a wealth of health benefits. Greek yogurt is rich in protein, calcium, and probiotics that promote gut health. The berries provide a dose of antioxidants and essential vitamins, while the mixed nuts contribute healthy fats and satisfying crunch. Plus, the low-carb nature of this breakfast makes it a perfect choice for those following a ketogenic lifestyle.

Take a moment to appreciate the vibrant colors and textures of this visually appealing breakfast creation. Allow each spoonful of the Greek Yogurt Parfait to transport you to the picturesque landscapes of Greece, where the sun-kissed flavors of the Mediterranean are brought to life.

So, why wait? Treat yourself to this delightful Greek Yogurt Parfait with Berries and Nuts and discover how a seemingly simple breakfast can be transformed into a keto Greek masterpiece. Embrace the flavors, nourish your body, and start your day with a burst of Mediterranean delight! Kali orexi (enjoy your meal)!

## Keto Spanakopita Quiche

Experience the unforgettable flavors of spanakopita in a keto-friendly form with this delectable Keto Spanakopita Quiche. Filled with the vibrant combination of spinach, feta cheese, and fragrant herbs, this Greek breakfast dish will transport you to the sunny hills of Greece while nourishing your body with wholesome, low-carb ingredients.

Ingredients:
- 1 pre-made keto-friendly pie crust (or homemade keto pie crust)
- 2 cups fresh spinach, chopped
- 1/2 cup crumbled feta cheese
- 4 large eggs
- 1/4 cup heavy cream
- 2 tablespoons chopped fresh dill
- 2 tablespoons chopped fresh parsley
- 1/4 teaspoon garlic powder
- Salt and pepper, to taste

Instructions:
1. Preheat the oven to 375°F (190°C).
2. Place the pre-made keto-friendly pie crust in a pie dish or tart pan, ensuring it is evenly spread along the bottom and sides.
3. In a skillet, sauté the chopped spinach over medium heat until wilted, about 2-3 minutes. Remove from heat and set aside.
4. In a mixing bowl, whisk together the eggs, heavy cream, garlic powder, chopped dill, and parsley. Season with salt and pepper to taste.
5. Spread the sautéed spinach evenly over the pie crust, followed by the crumbled feta cheese.
6. Pour the egg mixture over the spinach and feta, ensuring it is evenly distributed.
7. Place the quiche in the preheated oven and bake for 25-30 minutes, or until the quiche is set and the crust is golden brown.
8. Remove from the oven and let it cool for a few minutes before slicing and serving.
9. Enjoy the warm and savory Keto Spanakopita Quiche as a delightful Greek-inspired breakfast.

With its flavorful combination of spinach, feta cheese, and aromatic herbs, this Keto Spanakopita Quiche captures the essence of traditional spanakopita while keeping your carbohydrate intake low. The richness of the eggs and heavy cream contributes to a creamy texture, adding to the overall indulgence of this breakfast dish.

Savor each bite of the quiche as the flavors of Greece dance on your palate. Whether enjoyed freshly baked or as a reheated leftover, this keto twist on spanakopita will surely make your mornings memorable.

So, channel your inner Greek chef and let the aromas of the kitchen transport you to the sun-drenched shores of Greece. Delight in the flavors, embrace the keto lifestyle, and enjoy the wholesome goodness of this Keto Spanakopita Quiche. Truly a sublime way to start your day! Kali orexi!

## Keto Greek Breakfast Casserole

Awaken your senses and delight your taste buds with the comforting flavors of a Keto Greek Breakfast Casserole. This hearty and filling dish brings together classic Greek ingredients in a delicious, low-carb breakfast option that will keep you satisfied and energized throughout the morning.

Ingredients:
- 8 large eggs
- 1/4 cup heavy cream
- 1/2 cup diced bell peppers (assorted colors)
- 1/2 cup diced red onion
- 1/2 cup diced tomatoes
- 1/2 cup chopped Kalamata olives
- 1/2 cup crumbled feta cheese
- 1 teaspoon dried oregano
- Salt and pepper, to taste
- Fresh parsley, for garnish (optional)

Instructions:
1. Preheat the oven to 350°F (175°C) and lightly grease a baking dish.
2. In a large mixing bowl, whisk together the eggs and heavy cream until well combined. Season with salt, pepper, and dried oregano.
3. Add the diced bell peppers, red onion, tomatoes, chopped Kalamata olives, and crumbled feta cheese to the egg mixture. Mix well to ensure the ingredients are evenly distributed.
4. Pour the mixture into the prepared baking dish, spreading it out to create an even layer.
5. Bake in the preheated oven for 20-25 minutes, or until the casserole is set and the top is golden brown.
6. Remove from the oven and let it cool for a few minutes before garnishing with fresh parsley (if desired).
7. Slice into squares or wedges and serve warm.

This Keto Greek Breakfast Casserole is not only packed with flavor, but it also offers a wonderful balance of healthy fats, protein, and vegetables, making it a complete and satisfying meal. The combination of bell peppers, red onion, tomatoes, Kalamata olives, and feta cheese brings the essence of Greek cuisine to the forefront, creating a breakfast that is both nourishing and delicious.

This casserole is a versatile option that can be prepared ahead of time and reheated for quick and convenient breakfasts throughout the week. It can also be customized with your favorite keto-friendly additions, such as cooked bacon, spinach, or artichokes, to further enhance the flavors to suit your preferences.

So, whether you're hosting a brunch gathering or looking for a simple yet satisfying morning meal, this Keto Greek Breakfast Casserole is sure to impress. Embrace the flavors of Greece, fuel your body with wholesome ingredients, and savor the joys of a keto-friendly Greek breakfast. Kalí óreksi! Enjoy your meal!

## Keto Appetizers

Get ready to embark on a journey of tantalizing flavors and bite-sized delights as we delve into the world of Keto Appetizers in this chapter. Appetizers play a crucial role in Greek cuisine, offering a glimpse into the rich tapestry of flavors and ingredients that make up the Mediterranean culinary experience. By adapting these appetizers to align with the ketogenic diet, we can indulge in a variety of mouthwatering finger foods that are both low-carb and satisfying.

Greek appetizers, known as mezze, are a cultural tradition that goes beyond just satisfying our taste buds. These small plates bring people together, encouraging laughter, conversation, and a shared love for food. The vibrant assortment of flavors and textures found in Greek mezze showcases the diversity and abundance of the Mediterranean pantry, featuring ingredients like olive oil, fresh herbs, cheese, seafood, and vibrant seasonal vegetables.

In this chapter, we will explore a selection of keto-friendly Greek appetizer recipes that are sure to inspire your culinary creativity. From savory skewers and dips to crispy fritters and tantalizing salads, we will showcase the versatility and depth of Greek flavors while staying true to the principles of the ketogenic lifestyle.

By embracing the ketogenic diet, we can incorporate healthy fats, lean proteins, and low-carb vegetables into our appetizers, creating a balance of flavors and nutrients that will satiate our cravings while keeping our bodies in a state of ketosis. The recipes in this chapter will enable you to entertain guests, host Greek-inspired gatherings, or simply indulge in flavorful starters that bring a taste of Greece into your home.

Join us on this culinary adventure as we explore the art of creating keto Greek appetizers that are sure to impress and delight. From the tangy Tzatziki Dip with Veggie Sticks to the succulent Greek Lemon and Garlic Chicken Skewers, each recipe highlights the bold and unforgettable flavors of Greek cuisine transformed into keto-friendly masterpieces.

So, prepare your taste buds for a symphony of flavors, as we navigate through the vibrant world of Greek appetizers, reimagined for the ketogenic diet. Let's celebrate the joy of sharing and the pleasures of Greek cuisine, one delectable bite at a time. Yamas! Cheers to good food, good company, and a keto-friendly Mediterranean feast!

## Greek Lemon and Garlic Chicken Skewers

Transport your taste buds to the sunny shores of Greece with these mouthwatering Greek Lemon and Garlic Chicken Skewers. Bursting with Mediterranean flavors, this keto-friendly appetizer is a perfect combination of tender chicken, zesty lemon, aromatic garlic, and a harmonious blend of herbs and spices.

Ingredients:
- 1 pound boneless, skinless chicken breasts, cut into cubes
- 2 tablespoons freshly squeezed lemon juice
- 2 tablespoons olive oil
- 3 garlic cloves, minced
- 1 teaspoon dried oregano
- 1/2 teaspoon dried thyme
- 1/2 teaspoon dried rosemary
- Salt and pepper, to taste
- Wooden skewers, soaked in water for 30 minutes

Instructions:
1. In a bowl, combine the lemon juice, olive oil, minced garlic, dried oregano, dried thyme, dried rosemary, salt, and pepper. Mix well to create the marinade.
2. Add the chicken cubes to the marinade, ensuring they are evenly coated. Cover and refrigerate for at least 30 minutes to allow the flavors to meld.
3. Preheat the grill or grill pan to medium-high heat.
4. Thread the marinated chicken cubes onto the soaked wooden skewers.
5. Place the skewers on the preheated grill and cook for about 5-6 minutes per side, or until the chicken is cooked through and has a slight char.
6. Remove from the grill and let the skewers rest for a few minutes before serving.
7. Serve the Greek Lemon and Garlic Chicken Skewers as a keto-friendly appetizer, garnished with fresh herbs or a squeeze of lemon juice.

These Greek Lemon and Garlic Chicken Skewers are not only a flavorful keto appetizer but also a protein-packed delight. The combination of lemon, garlic, and herbs infuses the chicken with a vibrant Mediterranean essence, while the grilling process adds a delightful charred flavor that further enhances the experience.

Whether served at a casual gathering or as a special treat, these chicken skewers will impress your guests with their bold flavors and tender texture. Pair them with a refreshing tzatziki dip and a side of mixed Greek salad for a complete Mediterranean feast.

Delight in the joy of Greek cuisine, embrace the health benefits of a ketogenic lifestyle, and savor each succulent bite of these Greek Lemon and Garlic Chicken Skewers. Opa! Enjoy the fantastic flavors that Greece has to offer!

## Low-Carb Greek Salad Skewers

Experience the fresh and vibrant flavors of a classic Greek salad in a fun and bite-sized way with these Low-Carb Greek Salad Skewers. Packed with colorful vegetables, tangy feta cheese, and a zesty dressing, these keto-friendly skewers are perfect for parties, gatherings, or as a refreshing appetizer any time of the day.

Ingredients:
- Cherry tomatoes
- Cucumber, cut into cubes
- Red onion, cut into small wedges
- Kalamata olives
- Feta cheese, cut into cubes
- Fresh basil leaves
- Olive oil
- Red wine vinegar
- Dried oregano
- Salt and pepper, to taste
- Wooden skewers

Instructions:
1. Thread the cherry tomatoes, cucumber cubes, red onion wedges, Kalamata olives, feta cheese cubes, and fresh basil leaves alternately onto the wooden skewers.
2. In a small bowl, whisk together olive oil, red wine vinegar, dried oregano, salt, and pepper to create the dressing.
3. Drizzle the dressing over the skewers, ensuring they are evenly coated.
4. Arrange the Low-Carb Greek Salad Skewers on a platter and garnish with additional fresh basil leaves.
5. Serve and enjoy these delightful and flavorful keto Greek Salad Skewers.

These colorful and nutritious Low-Carb Greek Salad Skewers bring together all the components of a traditional Greek salad in a convenient and eye-catching form. The juicy cherry tomatoes, crisp cucumber, tangy feta cheese, and briny Kalamata olives, all threaded onto the skewers, provide a burst of flavor with every bite.

The dressing, with its combination of olive oil, red wine vinegar, and dried oregano, adds the signature Greek salad tanginess and aromatic touch to these skewers. With their vibrant presentation, they make a striking addition to any appetizer spread and are sure to be a hit among your guests.

Whether served as a prelude to a Greek-inspired feast or as a refreshing snack on a warm day, these Low-Carb Greek Salad Skewers embody the essence of Mediterranean flavors while adhering to your ketogenic lifestyle. So, embrace the taste of Greece, elevate your appetizer game, and enjoy the burst of freshness that these skewers bring to your palate. Opa!

## Keto Tzatziki Dip with Veggie Sticks

Indulge in the creamy and tangy flavors of Greece with this Keto Tzatziki Dip with Veggie Sticks. Made with Greek yogurt, cucumber, garlic, and fresh herbs, this refreshing dip is the perfect low-carb appetizer to satisfy your cravings while staying true to your ketogenic lifestyle.

Ingredients:
- 1 cup plain Greek yogurt
- 1/2 cucumber, grated and excess moisture squeezed out
- 2 garlic cloves, minced
- 1 tablespoon freshly squeezed lemon juice
- 1 tablespoon extra-virgin olive oil
- 1 tablespoon chopped fresh dill
- 1 tablespoon chopped fresh mint
- Salt and pepper, to taste
- Assorted vegetable sticks (carrots, celery, bell peppers, etc.) for dipping

Instructions:
1. In a bowl, combine the Greek yogurt, grated cucumber, minced garlic, lemon juice, extra-virgin olive oil, chopped dill, chopped mint, salt, and pepper. Mix well to ensure all ingredients are thoroughly incorporated.
2. Cover the bowl and refrigerate for at least 30 minutes to allow the flavors to meld.
3. Prior to serving, give the dip a stir and adjust the seasoning if desired.
4. Serve the Keto Tzatziki Dip with a selection of assorted vegetable sticks for dipping, such as carrots, celery, and bell peppers.
5. Enjoy the fresh and tangy flavors of this keto-friendly Tzatziki Dip and the crispness of the vegetable sticks.

This Keto Tzatziki Dip perfectly captures the essence of Greek cuisine with its creamy texture, refreshing cucumber, and fragrant herbs. The Greek yogurt provides a rich and creamy base while also offering probiotics and protein. The crisp and colorful vegetable sticks provide both a satisfying crunch and a nutritious accompaniment to the dip.

Whether you're hosting a gathering or simply treating yourself to a flavorful and healthy snack, this Keto Tzatziki Dip with Veggie Sticks is a versatile and satisfying appetizer option. The dip can be prepared in advance, allowing the flavors to meld and intensify, while the vegetable sticks provide a refreshing and low-carb alternative to traditional dippers.

So, dip into the vibrant flavors of Greece, elevate your appetizer game, and savor the delightful combination of creaminess, tanginess, and freshness of this Keto Tzatziki Dip. Opa! Enjoy the vibrant flavors and healthy indulgence that Greek cuisine has to offer while staying in line with your ketogenic journey!

## Greek Zucchini Balls (Kolokithokeftedes)

Elevate your appetizer game with these delicious and keto-friendly Greek Zucchini Balls, also known as Kolokithokeftedes. These crispy and flavorful bites showcase the versatility of zucchini and the aromatic herbs of Greek cuisine, making them a perfect addition to any Mediterranean-inspired spread.

Ingredients:
- 2 medium zucchini, grated
- 1/2 teaspoon salt
- 2 green onions, finely chopped
- 1/4 cup chopped fresh parsley
- 2 tablespoons chopped fresh dill
- 1/4 cup crumbled feta cheese
- 1/4 cup almond flour
- 1 large egg
- 1/4 teaspoon garlic powder
- Salt and pepper, to taste
- Olive oil, for frying

Instructions:
1. Place the grated zucchini in a colander, sprinkle with salt, and let it sit for about 10 minutes. This will help draw out excess moisture from the zucchini.
2. Squeeze the grated zucchini to remove as much moisture as possible, then transfer it to a clean, dry kitchen towel. Wrap the towel around the zucchini and squeeze again to remove any remaining liquid.
3. In a mixing bowl, combine the grated zucchini, green onions, parsley, dill, crumbled feta cheese, almond flour, egg, garlic powder, salt, and pepper. Mix well until all ingredients are evenly incorporated.
4. Heat a generous amount of olive oil in a large non-stick frying pan over medium heat.
5. Scoop tablespoon-sized portions of the zucchini mixture and shape them into balls using your hands.
6. Place the zucchini balls carefully into the hot oil, allowing them to fry for about 3-4 minutes on each side until golden brown and crispy.
7. Once cooked, transfer the zucchini balls to a paper towel-lined plate to absorb any excess oil.
8. Serve the Greek Zucchini Balls (Kolokithokeftedes) as a delightful and keto-friendly appetizer, accompanied by a side of tzatziki sauce or a squeeze of lemon juice.

These Greek Zucchini Balls offer a harmonious combination of flavors and textures. The zucchini brings a mild and refreshing taste, while the fresh herbs, feta cheese, and garlic elevate the flavors to a whole new level. The almond flour acts as a binder and gives the zucchini balls their desired crispiness.

Whether served as a stand-alone appetizer or as part of a mezze platter, these zucchini balls make a delightful addition to any gathering or simply a tasty snack. They offer a creative and healthy way to enjoy the goodness of zucchini while staying committed to your ketogenic journey.

So, embrace the flavors and traditions of Greek cuisine, delight your taste buds with these Greek Zucchini Balls, and enjoy the irresistible combination of crispy, cheesy, and herb-infused bites. Opa! Experience the authentic taste of Greece with every mouthwatering morsel!

## Soups and Salads

Get ready to embark on a culinary journey through the comforting world of Greek soups and the refreshing realm of Greek salads. In this chapter, we will explore the vibrant flavors, wholesome ingredients, and traditional Greek techniques that make these dishes a staple in Greek cuisine. And the best part? We will do it all while staying true to our ketogenic lifestyle.

Greek cuisine is renowned for showcasing the bounties of the Mediterranean, with dishes that celebrate fresh, seasonal produce, aromatic herbs, and the harmonious marriage of flavors. In this chapter, we will discover how to adapt these classic Greek soups and salads to fit within the guidelines of the ketogenic diet, without sacrificing the rich taste and cultural essence that makes them special.

From creamy and comforting soups to vibrant and nutrient-packed salads, Greek cuisine offers a wide range of options to tantalize your taste buds and nourish your body. As we delve into this chapter, we will learn to embrace the flavors of Greece while adhering to our low-carb, high-fat way of eating.

In the soup section, we will explore traditional Greek recipes such as Avgolemono, a velvety and tangy lemon-egg soup, and Stuffed Pepper Soup, a hearty and satisfying dish bursting with Mediterranean flavors. These soups will warm your soul and provide you with nourishment and comfort on a keto journey.

Moving on to the salad section, we will dive into vibrant bowls of goodness that reflect the colors of the Greek countryside. From the classic Greek Salad with its crisp cucumbers, juicy tomatoes, tangy feta, and briny olives, to creative takes on salads using low-carb ingredients and fresh herbs, we will discover how to create salads that are both visually stunning and satisfying to the palate.

Prepare to awaken your senses as we explore the art of crafting Greek soups that comfort and salads that invigorate, all while adhering to the principles of a ketogenic lifestyle. Throughout this chapter, we will celebrate the abundance of the Mediterranean diet and its ability to nourish our bodies and delight our taste buds.

So, whether you're looking for warming soup recipes to enjoy on a cozy evening or vibrant salads to accompany your main dishes, this chapter will guide you in creating authentic Greek flavors with a keto twist. Let's embrace the magic of Greek soups and salads, elevate our ketogenic experience, and embark on a journey of health and culinary discovery. Yamas! Cheers to embracing the richness of Greek cuisine in a low-carb and flavor-packed way!

## Creamy Keto Avgolemono Soup

Indulge in the velvety richness of a Creamy Keto Avgolemono Soup, a classic Greek delicacy that combines the vibrant flavors of lemon and egg with a comforting, creamy base. This keto-friendly adaptation of the traditional Avgolemono soup will transport you to the sunny shores of Greece while keeping you in line with your low-carb, high-fat lifestyle.

Ingredients:
- 4 cups chicken broth (preferably homemade or low-sodium)
- 1/2 cup cooked chicken, shredded or diced
- 3 large eggs
- Juice of 2 lemons
- Zest of 1 lemon
- Salt and pepper, to taste
- Fresh dill, for garnish (optional)

Instructions:
1. In a large pot, bring the chicken broth to a gentle simmer over medium heat.
2. Add the cooked chicken to the pot and simmer for a few minutes until heated through.
3. In a mixing bowl, whisk together the eggs, lemon juice, and lemon zest until well combined.
4. Slowly ladle about 1 cup of the hot broth into the egg mixture, whisking continuously to temper the eggs.
5. Gradually pour the egg mixture back into the pot, whisking constantly to ensure even distribution.
6. Continue cooking over low heat, stirring gently with a wooden spoon, until the soup thickens slightly, about 3-4 minutes.
7. Season with salt and pepper to taste. Note: Be careful not to let the soup boil, as it may cause the eggs to curdle.
8. Remove from heat and ladle the Creamy Keto Avgolemono Soup into bowls.
9. Garnish with fresh dill, if desired.
10. Serve hot, savor the tangy creaminess of the soup, and enjoy the keto-friendly version of this Greek classic.

The Creamy Keto Avgolemono Soup offers a perfect balance of tangy lemon, creamy texture, and comforting flavors. With the protein-packed chicken and the richness of eggs, this soup provides a satisfying and nourishing meal that will keep you satiated throughout the day.

Allow the essence of Greek cuisine to transport you to picturesque tavernas overlooking the Mediterranean Sea. Close your eyes, take a spoonful of the Creamy Keto Avgolemono Soup, and relish the harmonious blend of flavors that make Greek food so beloved around the world.

So, bring the richness and tangy allure of Greece into your kitchen with this delightful Creamy Keto Avgolemono Soup. Nourish your body with wholesome ingredients, indulge in the Mediterranean experience, and embrace the keto lifestyle with every spoonful. Kali orexi! Enjoy your meal!

## Greek Cucumber Salad with Feta and Olives

Cool, refreshing, and bursting with Mediterranean flavors, the Greek Cucumber Salad with Feta and Olives is a vibrant addition to any meal. This keto-friendly rendition of a classic Greek salad will transport your taste buds to the sun-kissed beaches of Greece with every crisp bite.

Ingredients:
- 2 large cucumbers, peeled and thinly sliced
- 1 cup cherry tomatoes, halved
- 1/2 cup Kalamata olives, pitted and halved
- 1/2 cup crumbled feta cheese
- 2 tablespoons extra virgin olive oil
- 1 tablespoon fresh lemon juice
- 1 tablespoon chopped fresh dill
- Salt and pepper, to taste

Instructions:
1. In a salad bowl, combine the sliced cucumbers, halved cherry tomatoes, Kalamata olives, and crumbled feta cheese.
2. Drizzle the extra virgin olive oil and lemon juice over the salad ingredients.
3. Sprinkle the chopped fresh dill on top.
4. Season with salt and pepper to taste.
5. Gently toss all the ingredients until well combined and coated with the dressing.
6. Let the Greek Cucumber Salad sit for a few minutes to allow the flavors to meld together.
7. Serve chilled, and revel in the refreshing flavors of Greece with this keto-friendly salad.

The Greek Cucumber Salad with Feta and Olives is a perfect embodiment of the Mediterranean diet, with its abundance of fresh vegetables, briny olives, and tangy feta cheese. This salad not only offers a burst of flavors but also provides a satisfying crunch and a wealth of nutrients.

Take a moment to appreciate the vibrant colors and textures of this Greek salad masterpiece. Each bite brings together the crispness of cucumber, the juicy burst of cherry tomatoes, the tangy bite of Kalamata olives, and the creamy goodness of feta cheese. The combination of extra virgin olive oil, lemon juice, and dill adds a refreshing and aromatic touch, elevating the salad to new heights of deliciousness.

Whether enjoyed as a refreshing side dish or as a light and satisfying meal on its own, this Greek Cucumber Salad with Feta and Olives brings the taste of the Mediterranean to your table. So, embrace the flavors, take a bite, and let this keto-friendly salad transport you to the warm shores of Greece, even if just for a moment. Kalí óreksi! Enjoy your meal!

## Keto Greek Salad with Grilled Chicken

Elevate your salad game with the Keto Greek Salad with Grilled Chicken, a satisfying and nutrient-packed dish that showcases the vibrant flavors of Greece. This low-carb adaptation of the classic Greek salad incorporates juicy grilled chicken to create a complete and satisfying meal that will leave you feeling nourished and energized.

Ingredients:
- 8 oz chicken breast, boneless and skinless
- 4 cups mixed salad greens (such as romaine, spinach, and arugula)
- 1 cup cherry tomatoes, halved
- 1/2 cup diced cucumber
- 1/4 cup sliced red onion
- 1/4 cup pitted Kalamata olives
- 1/4 cup crumbled feta cheese
- 2 tablespoons extra virgin olive oil
- 1 tablespoon fresh lemon juice
- 1 teaspoon dried oregano
- Salt and pepper, to taste

Instructions:
1. Preheat the grill or grill pan over medium-high heat.
2. Season the chicken breast with salt, pepper, and dried oregano.
3. Grill the chicken for 6-8 minutes per side, or until cooked through. Allow it to rest for a few minutes before slicing it into thin strips.
4. In a large salad bowl, combine the mixed salad greens, cherry tomatoes, diced cucumber, sliced red onion, Kalamata olives, and crumbled feta cheese.
5. Drizzle the extra virgin olive oil and lemon juice over the salad ingredients.
6. Season with salt and pepper to taste.
7. Toss the salad gently to coat all the ingredients with the dressing.
8. Arrange the grilled chicken strips on top of the salad.
9. Serve immediately, and revel in the flavors of Greece with this hearty and satisfying Keto Greek Salad with Grilled Chicken.

The Keto Greek Salad with Grilled Chicken takes the traditional Greek salad to a whole new level by adding tender and flavorful grilled chicken. This addition not only enhances the protein content of the dish but also provides a delicious and satiating element that turns the salad into a complete meal.

The combination of fresh salad greens, juicy cherry tomatoes, crisp cucumber, piquant red onion, briny Kalamata olives, and tangy feta cheese creates a symphony of flavors and textures. The dressing, made with extra virgin olive oil and fresh lemon juice, adds a zesty and Mediterranean touch that ties all the ingredients together.

Embrace the beauty of Greek cuisine with this Keto Greek Salad with Grilled Chicken. Enjoy the harmony of flavors, the vibrant colors, and the satisfaction of a well-rounded, low-carb meal. Whether enjoyed for lunch or dinner, this salad is a testament to the nourishing and delicious possibilities of combining the principles of the ketogenic diet with the vibrant flavors of Greece. Kali orexi! Enjoy your meal!

## Low-Carb Stuffed Pepper Soup

Indulge in the comforting flavors of stuffed peppers with a twist in this Low-Carb Stuffed Pepper Soup. Laden with tender bell peppers, ground meat, tomatoes, and aromatic herbs, this hearty keto-friendly soup will warm your soul and transport you to the vibrant kitchens of Greece.

Ingredients:
- 1 lb ground beef (or turkey, chicken, or a combination)
- 2 bell peppers, any color, diced
- 1 small onion, diced
- 2 cloves garlic, minced
- 1 can (14 oz) diced tomatoes
- 4 cups beef or vegetable broth (preferably homemade or low-sodium)
- 1 tablespoon tomato paste
- 1 teaspoon dried basil
- 1 teaspoon dried oregano
- 1/2 teaspoon dried thyme
- Salt and pepper, to taste

Instructions:
1. In a large pot or Dutch oven, brown the ground beef over medium heat until fully cooked. Drain any excess grease if necessary.
2. Add the diced bell peppers, onion, and garlic to the pot. Sauté for 5-7 minutes until the vegetables soften.
3. Stir in the diced tomatoes, beef or vegetable broth, and tomato paste.
4. Add the dried basil, dried oregano, dried thyme, salt, and pepper. Stir well to combine.
5. Bring the soup to a boil, then reduce the heat to low. Cover and simmer for 20-25 minutes, allowing the flavors to meld together.
6. Taste and adjust the seasoning if necessary.
7. Serve hot and savor the comforting flavors of this Low-Carb Stuffed Pepper Soup.

This Low-Carb Stuffed Pepper Soup captures the essence of stuffed peppers in a soul-warming bowl. The combination of ground meat, tender bell peppers, aromatic herbs, and flavorful tomatoes evokes the comforting and satisfying flavors of the classic dish.

Each spoonful of this soup brings you the savory delight of stuffed peppers, while keeping the carbs in check. Its richness and heartiness make it a perfect keto-friendly option to enjoy on a chilly evening or as a comforting lunch.

Embrace the flavors of Greece in this comforting Low-Carb Stuffed Pepper Soup. Immerse yourself in the warmth and aroma of the Mediterranean, and allow the nourishing ingredients and vibrant flavors to soothe your senses. Kali orexi! Enjoy your meal!

## Mains and Sides

Welcome to Chapter 5 of our keto Greek recipe journey, where we dive into the heart of Greek cuisine. In this chapter, we explore a wide array of main dishes and sides that will transport you to the tavernas of Greece and satisfy your cravings for bold flavors and comforting meals. From traditional favorites to innovative creations, you'll discover how Greek cuisine can seamlessly integrate into your ketogenic lifestyle.

Greek cuisine is known for its diverse range of main dishes and sides that showcase the vibrant flavors of the Mediterranean. From succulent grilled meats and seafood to hearty vegetable-based dishes, the Greek culinary tradition has something to offer for every palate. And what's more exciting is that we've adapted these timeless recipes to align with the principles of the ketogenic diet.

In this chapter, get ready to embark on a gastronomic adventure as we introduce you to a variety of keto Greek main dishes and sides. We'll explore the art of balancing the unique flavors of Greek herbs and spices with the satiating power of healthy fats and quality proteins, creating dishes that are both satisfying and nourishing.

Imagine sinking your teeth into tender lemon-infused grilled chicken souvlaki or indulging in a comforting keto moussaka with layers of eggplant, ground meat, and creamy béchamel sauce. These are just a taste of what awaits you in this section. And let's not forget the array of sides, such as stuffed bell peppers bursting with Mediterranean goodness or Greek-style zucchini balls (Kolokithokeftedes) offering a delightful crunch.

No matter your dietary preferences, this chapter has something for everyone. These recipes will not only tantalize your taste buds but also provide you with a complete, well-balanced meal that adheres to your ketogenic goals.

So, whether you're searching for a cozy, family-friendly dinner idea or planning an impressive feast for guests, the main dishes and side recipes in this chapter will guide you toward creating unforgettable meals that celebrate the essence of Greek cuisine while keeping you firmly on the path of the ketogenic lifestyle.

Get ready to immerse yourself in the flavors, aromas, and rich traditions of Greek cuisine as we journey through these enticing keto Greek main dishes and sides. Prepare to delight in the marriage of robust ingredients, burst of Mediterranean herbs, and the magic that happens when Greek flavors meet the ketogenic way of eating.

So, tie on your apron, channel your inner Greek chef, and let's dive into Chapter 5, where the captivating and fulfilling world of keto Greek mains and sides awaits. Kali orexi! Enjoy your meal!

## Lemon and Herb Grilled Chicken Souvlaki

Transport yourself to the sun-soaked Mediterranean shores with this tantalizing Lemon and Herb Grilled Chicken Souvlaki. Bursting with Greek flavors and marinated to perfection, this keto Greek main dish will satisfy your cravings for succulent, charred chicken infused with vibrant herbs and zesty citrus.

Ingredients:
- 1.5 pounds boneless, skinless chicken breasts, cut into bite-sized pieces
- 1/4 cup extra-virgin olive oil
- Juice of 1 lemon
- Zest of 1 lemon
- 2 cloves garlic, minced
- 1 tablespoon chopped fresh oregano
- 1 tablespoon chopped fresh parsley
- 1 teaspoon dried thyme
- Salt and pepper, to taste
- Skewers, for grilling

Instructions:
1. In a bowl, whisk together the olive oil, lemon juice, lemon zest, minced garlic, chopped oregano, chopped parsley, dried thyme, salt, and pepper to prepare the marinade.
2. Add the chicken pieces to the marinade and toss until well coated. Allow the chicken to marinate in the refrigerator for at least 30 minutes, or ideally, up to 24 hours for maximum flavor infusion.
3. Preheat your grill or grill pan to medium-high heat.
4. Thread the marinated chicken pieces onto skewers, ensuring they are evenly distributed.
5. Grill the chicken skewers for about 4-5 minutes per side, or until the chicken is cooked through and has beautiful grill marks.
6. Remove the chicken skewers from the grill and let them rest for a few minutes before serving.
7. Serve the Lemon and Herb Grilled Chicken Souvlaki hot, garnished with fresh parsley for an extra pop of color and flavor.

The Lemon and Herb Grilled Chicken Souvlaki embraces the traditional Greek technique of marinating meat to infuse it with incredible taste. The combination of fresh lemon juice and zest, aromatic herbs like oregano and parsley, and the rich flavor of garlic creates a marinade that elevates the grilled chicken to a whole new level of deliciousness.

This dish pairs perfectly with a refreshing Greek salad or a side of tzatziki sauce for dipping. The zesty and herb-infused chicken, combined with the vibrant flavors of Greek cuisine, will transport you to the sun-drenched terraces of Greece with every bite.

Whether grilling outdoors or using a grill pan indoors, this Lemon and Herb Grilled Chicken Souvlaki is perfect for a relaxed family dinner or outdoor get-together with friends. Embrace the joy of the Mediterranean flavors and savor the satisfaction of enjoying a keto Greek main dish that nourishes your body and delights your taste buds.

So, fire up the grill, thread the marinated chicken onto skewers, and let the aroma of this Greek-inspired masterpiece fill the air. Get ready to experience the irresistible allure of Lemon and Herb Grilled Chicken Souvlaki, keto-style. Kali orexi!

## Keto Moussaka with Eggplant

Experience the Greek classic like never before with this delightful Keto Moussaka with Eggplant. Layered with rich flavors, tender eggplant, and a creamy béchamel sauce, this low-carb twist on the traditional moussaka will transport you to the cozy tavernas of Greece with every mouthwatering bite.

Ingredients:
- 2 large eggplants, sliced lengthwise into 1/4-inch thick slices
- 1 pound ground meat (beef, lamb, or a combination)
- 1/2 cup diced onion
- 2 cloves garlic, minced
- 1 can (14 ounces) diced tomatoes
- 2 tablespoons tomato paste
- 1 teaspoon dried oregano
- 1/2 teaspoon ground cinnamon
- Salt and pepper, to taste
- 1/4 cup grated Parmesan cheese
- Fresh parsley, for garnish (optional)

For the Béchamel Sauce:
- 2 tablespoons unsalted butter
- 2 tablespoons almond flour
- 3/4 cup heavy cream
- 1/4 cup grated Parmesan cheese
- 2 large eggs, lightly beaten
- Salt and pepper, to taste

Instructions:
1. Preheat the oven to 400°F (200°C). Lay the eggplant slices on a baking sheet and brush both sides with olive oil. Bake for about 10 minutes per side until slightly softened and golden. Set aside.
2. In a large skillet over medium heat, cook the ground meat, diced onion, and minced garlic until the meat is browned and the onions are softened.
3. Stir in the diced tomatoes, tomato paste, dried oregano, ground cinnamon, salt, and pepper. Simmer for about 10-15 minutes, allowing the flavors to meld together.
4. Meanwhile, prepare the béchamel sauce. In a separate saucepan, melt the butter over medium heat. Stir in the almond flour until well combined to create a roux.
5. Slowly pour in the heavy cream, whisking continuously to avoid lumps. Cook until the sauce thickens. Remove from heat and stir in the grated Parmesan cheese, beaten eggs, salt, and pepper.
6. Grease a baking dish and arrange half of the eggplant slices in a single layer. Spread half of the meat mixture on top, followed by another layer of the remaining eggplant slices.
7. Pour the béchamel sauce over the top, ensuring it covers the entire surface. Sprinkle with grated Parmesan cheese.
8. Bake in the preheated oven for 25-30 minutes or until the moussaka is golden brown and bubbling.

9. Remove from the oven and let it cool for a few minutes before garnishing with fresh parsley (if desired).
10. Slice into portions and serve warm, savoring the complex layers of flavors.

This Keto Moussaka with Eggplant offers all the rich and comforting flavors of the traditional dish while staying true to the principles of the ketogenic diet. The tender, roasted eggplant serves as a luscious base for the hearty meat filling, and the creamy béchamel sauce perfectly ties all the flavors together.

Serve this delectable moussaka with a side of Greek salad to complete your keto Greek feast. The blend of ground meat, aromatic herbs, and creamy Parmesan-infused layers will transport you to the heart of Greece from the comfort of your own home.

Celebrate the captivating flavors of Greece with this Keto Moussaka with Eggplant, embracing the richness and depth of traditional Greek cuisine in a low-carb, keto-friendly format. Immerse yourself in the comfort of this classic dish, and prepare to nourish your body and delight your taste buds in the most satisfying way. Kali orexi!

# Greek Style Stuffed Bell Peppers

Elevate your dining experience with the vibrant flavors of Greek Style Stuffed Bell Peppers. This keto Greek side dish brings together the natural sweetness of bell peppers and a deliciously seasoned filling, creating a harmonious blend of textures and tastes that will impress even the most discerning palate.

Ingredients:
- 4 large bell peppers (assorted colors), tops removed and seeds removed
- 1 pound ground meat (beef, turkey, or chicken)
- 1/2 cup diced onion
- 2 cloves garlic, minced
- 1/2 cup diced tomatoes
- 1/4 cup chopped fresh parsley
- 1 teaspoon dried oregano
- 1/2 teaspoon ground cinnamon
- Salt and pepper, to taste
- 1/4 cup crumbled feta cheese, for topping
- Fresh parsley, for garnish

Instructions:
1. Preheat the oven to 375°F (190°C). Grease a baking dish that will snugly fit the bell peppers.
2. In a large skillet over medium heat, cook the ground meat, diced onion, and minced garlic until the meat is browned and the onions are translucent.
3. Add the diced tomatoes, chopped parsley, dried oregano, ground cinnamon, salt, and pepper. Stir well to combine and simmer for 5-7 minutes to allow the flavors to meld together.
4. Fill each bell pepper with the meat mixture, pressing it down gently and filling it to the top.
5. Place the stuffed bell peppers in the greased baking dish. If any bell peppers have a tendency to tilt, use a small piece of aluminum foil to stabilize them.
6. Cover the baking dish with foil and bake for 30 minutes.
7. After 30 minutes, remove the foil and sprinkle the crumbled feta cheese on top of each bell pepper. Return to the oven and bake for an additional 10-15 minutes until the peppers are tender and the cheese is melted and golden.
8. Remove from the oven and let them cool for a few minutes. Garnish with fresh parsley before serving.

These Greek Style Stuffed Bell Peppers demonstrate the art of combining simple, wholesome ingredients to create a dish that is both satisfying and impressive. The tender bell peppers provide a sweet and vibrant vessel for the well-seasoned meat filling, while the crumbled feta cheese adds a tangy finish that perfectly complements the other flavors.

These stuffed bell peppers can be enjoyed as a satisfying side dish or as a standalone meal. Serve them alongside a fresh Greek salad or with a side of cauliflower rice to complete your keto Greek feast. The explosion of Mediterranean-inspired flavors will transport you to the charming seaside villages of Greece, where the taste of tradition and the allure of the keto lifestyle collide.

So, invite your loved ones to gather around the table, savor the joy of Greek flavors, and relish in the pleasure of Greek Style Stuffed Bell Peppers. Experience the sophistication and simplicity of Greek cuisine in every delicious bite. Kali orexi!

# Keto Greek Stuffed Chicken Breast

Elevate your keto Greek culinary adventures with this exquisite Keto Greek Stuffed Chicken Breast. Packed with Mediterranean-inspired flavors and filled with a delicious combination of spinach, feta cheese, and aromatic herbs, this dish is a true showstopper that will impress your taste buds and leave you satisfied.

Ingredients:
- 4 boneless, skinless chicken breasts
- 1 cup fresh spinach, chopped
- 1/2 cup crumbled feta cheese
- 2 tablespoons chopped fresh dill
- 2 tablespoons chopped fresh parsley
- 2 cloves garlic, minced
- 1 tablespoon lemon juice
- 2 tablespoons extra-virgin olive oil
- Salt and pepper, to taste
- Cooking twine, for securing the stuffed chicken breasts

Instructions:
1. Preheat the oven to 375°F (190°C).
2. In a small mixing bowl, combine the chopped spinach, crumbled feta cheese, chopped dill, chopped parsley, minced garlic, lemon juice, and olive oil. Mix well to create the stuffing mixture.
3. Carefully slice a pocket in each chicken breast by making a horizontal cut along the side, being careful not to cut all the way through.
4. Generously stuff each chicken breast with the mixture, ensuring that the filling is evenly distributed.
5. Use cooking twine to tie each stuffed chicken breast securely, holding the filling in place.
6. Season the outside of the chicken breasts with salt and pepper.
7. Heat a non-stick skillet over medium-high heat. Place the stuffed chicken breasts in the skillet and sear for about 2-3 minutes on each side until golden brown.
8. Transfer the seared chicken breasts onto a baking sheet lined with parchment paper. Bake in the preheated oven for 20-25 minutes or until the chicken is cooked through.
9. Remove from the oven and let the stuffed chicken breasts rest for a few minutes before removing the twine.
10. Slice the chicken breasts crosswise into attractive rounds and serve warm, garnished with fresh herbs if desired.

The Keto Greek Stuffed Chicken Breast takes the humble chicken breast to new heights, infusing it with vibrant Mediterranean flavors. The combination of spinach, feta cheese, fresh herbs, and tangy lemon juice results in a delightful burst of taste and texture. The searing process creates a delicious golden crust, while baking the chicken ensures a tender and juicy interior.

Serve the stuffed chicken breasts alongside a crisp Greek salad or a side of roasted vegetables for a complete Greek-inspired meal that will transport you to the sun-soaked islands of Greece. The intricate flavors and innovative use of ingredients highlight the beauty and creativity of Greek cuisine while adhering to the principles of the ketogenic lifestyle.

So, bring the flavors of Greece to your table, unravel the aromatic layers, and experience pure culinary bliss with this Keto Greek Stuffed Chicken Breast. Enjoy the fusion of succulent chicken, vibrant fillings, and the harmony of keto Greek ingredients. Kali orexi! Enjoy your meal!

# Greek Desserts

Indulge in the sweet allure of Greek desserts while staying true to your ketogenic lifestyle with the delightful creations in this chapter. Greek desserts are known for their rich flavors, enticing aromas, and unique combinations of ingredients. In this chapter, we will explore how to adapt these traditional delights into keto-friendly versions that satisfy your sweet tooth without derailing your dietary goals.

Greek desserts are a celebration of heritage and culture, often inspired by the ancient recipes that have been passed down through generations. From the iconic Baklava to the creamy Galaktoboureko and the irresistible Loukoumades, Greek desserts offer a tantalizing array of options for those with a sweet tooth.

The challenge lies in transforming these beloved treats into low-carb, high-fat versions while preserving their essence and decadence. By making smart ingredient choices and employing keto-friendly alternatives, we can recreate the flavors and textures that make Greek desserts so special.

In this chapter, we will explore a variety of keto Greek dessert recipes that will transport you to the sun-drenched shores of Greece. From the richness of a Baklava Cheesecake Bar to the smoothness of Greek Yogurt Panna Cotta, each recipe is crafted to deliver the satisfaction of traditional Greek desserts without compromising your ketogenic lifestyle.

By utilizing ingredients such as almond flour, coconut flour, natural keto sweeteners, and healthy fats like coconut oil and heavy cream, we can recreate the delicious flavors and textures that make Greek desserts a true delight. These keto Greek desserts not only satisfy your cravings but also provide a source of nourishment and pleasure in each bite.

Bring the enchanting Mediterranean flavors into your kitchen, embracing the challenge of making Greek desserts compatible with your keto journey. Whether you're preparing them for special occasions, entertaining guests, or simply treating yourself to a guilt-free indulgence, these recipes will ignite your taste buds and transport you to the heart of Greek culinary euphoria.

So, get ready to embark on a culinary adventure through the sweet side of Greek cuisine. Let's delve into the world of mouthwatering Greek desserts, transformed into keto-friendly delights. Savor the flavors, delight in the textures, and satisfy your cravings while celebrating the best of both worlds. Embrace the richness of Greek desserts, keto-style. Kalí óreksi! Enjoy your sweet journey!

## Keto Baklava Cheesecake Bars

Satisfy your craving for the iconic Greek dessert, Baklava, with a keto-friendly twist in these delectable Keto Baklava Cheesecake Bars. Indulge in the heavenly combination of buttery nut layers, sweet syrup, and creamy cheesecake, all while keeping your carbohydrate intake in check. Get ready to experience the flavors of Baklava in a guilt-free and keto-friendly delight.

Ingredients:
For the Crust:
- 1 ½ cups almond flour
- ¼ cup coconut flour
- 1/3 cup granulated keto sweetener
- ½ teaspoon ground cinnamon
- ¼ teaspoon salt
- ½ cup unsalted butter, melted

For the Cheesecake Filling:
- 16 oz cream cheese, softened
- ½ cup granulated keto sweetener
- 2 large eggs
- 1 teaspoon vanilla extract
- 1 tablespoon lemon juice

For the Nut Topping:
- 1 cup mixed chopped nuts (such as walnuts, almonds, and pistachios)
- 2 tablespoons granulated keto sweetener
- ½ teaspoon ground cinnamon

For the Syrup:
- ¼ cup water
- ¼ cup granulated keto sweetener
- 2 tablespoons honey alternative (such as sugar-free honey or a keto-friendly syrup)
- 1 tablespoon lemon juice
- 1 teaspoon rose water (optional)

Instructions:
1. Preheat the oven to 325°F (165°C) and line a square baking dish with parchment paper, ensuring it extends over the sides for easy removal.
2. In a mixing bowl, combine the almond flour, coconut flour, sweetener, ground cinnamon, and salt for the crust. Stir in the melted butter until a crumbly mixture forms.
3. Press the crust mixture evenly into the bottom of the prepared baking dish.
4. Bake the crust in the preheated oven for 10 minutes, then remove and set aside.
5. In a separate bowl, beat the softened cream cheese with the sweetener until smooth and well combined.
6. Add the eggs, one at a time, followed by the vanilla extract and lemon juice, mixing until smooth and creamy.
7. Pour the cheesecake filling over the baked crust, spreading it evenly.

8. In a small bowl, combine the chopped nuts, sweetener, and ground cinnamon for the nut topping. Sprinkle the nut mixture over the cheesecake filling.
9. Return the baking dish to the oven and bake for 25-30 minutes, or until the cheesecake is set and the edges are slightly golden.
10. While the cheesecake bakes, prepare the syrup. In a saucepan, combine the water, sweetener, honey alternative, lemon juice, and rose water (if using). Bring to a gentle boil over medium heat, then reduce the heat and simmer for 5 minutes until the syrup thickens slightly.
11. Remove the cheesecake from the oven and allow it to cool for a few minutes. Pour the syrup evenly over the top of the warm cheesecake.
12. Let the cheesecake cool completely in the baking dish before transferring to the refrigerator to chill for at least 4 hours, or overnight.
13. Once chilled, use the parchment paper to lift the cheesecake out of the dish. Cut into squares and serve your irresistible Keto Baklava Cheesecake Bars.

Enjoy the incredible flavors and textures of traditional Baklava without compromising your ketogenic lifestyle. These Baklava Cheesecake Bars offer a harmonious balance of rich nuttiness, sweet syrup, and creamy cheesecake, all within the framework of low-carb ingredients and natural keto sweeteners.

Every bite will take you on a journey through the captivating tastes of Greece, leaving you satisfied and craving-free. Share these Keto Baklava Cheesecake Bars with friends and family, or keep them all to yourself as a guilt-free indulgence.

Experience the magic of Baklava reimagined for the ketogenic lifestyle. Get ready to fall in love with the melt-in-your-mouth texture, enticing nutty aroma, and sweet symphony of flavors in these delectable Keto Baklava Cheesecake Bars. Opa!

## Greek Yogurt Panna Cotta with Berry Sauce

Savor a smooth and velvety Greek Yogurt Panna Cotta topped with a vibrant berry sauce, creating a stunning keto Greek dessert that will captivate your taste buds. This luscious treat combines the creamy goodness of Greek yogurt with the natural sweetness of berries, resulting in a refreshing and satisfying dessert that is both indulgent and guilt-free.

Ingredients:
For the Panna Cotta:
- 2 cups full-fat Greek yogurt
- 1 cup heavy cream
- 1/4 cup powdered keto sweetener
- 1 teaspoon vanilla extract
- 2 1/2 teaspoons powdered gelatin
- 2 tablespoons cold water

For the Berry Sauce:
- 1 cup mixed berries (such as strawberries, blueberries, and raspberries)
- 1 tablespoon powdered keto sweetener
- 1 tablespoon lemon juice
- Fresh mint leaves, for garnish (optional)

Instructions:
For the Panna Cotta:
1. In a small bowl, sprinkle the gelatin over the cold water and let it bloom for 5 minutes.
2. In a saucepan, heat the heavy cream over medium heat until hot but not boiling. Remove from heat.
3. Add the bloomed gelatin to the hot cream, stirring until completely dissolved.
4. In a separate mixing bowl, whisk together the Greek yogurt, powdered sweetener, and vanilla extract until smooth.
5. Slowly pour the cream mixture into the yogurt mixture, whisking continuously until well combined and smooth.
6. Divide the mixture among serving glasses or ramekins. Chill in the refrigerator for at least 4 hours, or until set.

For the Berry Sauce:
1. In a blender or food processor, combine the mixed berries, powdered sweetener, and lemon juice. Blend until smooth and well combined.
2. Pass the berry mixture through a fine-mesh sieve to remove any seeds or pulp, if desired.
3. Refrigerate the berry sauce until ready to use.

To Assemble:
1. Once the panna cotta has set, remove it from the refrigerator.
2. Spoon a generous amount of the chilled berry sauce over each panna cotta.
3. Garnish with fresh mint leaves, if desired, for an extra pop of color and freshness.
4. Serve chilled and enjoy the smooth and tangy delight of Greek Yogurt Panna Cotta with Berry Sauce.

This Greek-inspired dessert allows you to indulge in creamy decadence while staying true to your ketogenic lifestyle. The velvety texture of Greek yogurt combined with the vibrant burst of flavors from the berry sauce creates a harmonious and refreshing dessert that will leave you feeling satisfied and utterly delighted.

Whether enjoyed as an elegant conclusion to a meal or a special treat at any time of day, this Greek Yogurt Panna Cotta with Berry Sauce is sure to impress. Immerse yourself in the flavors of Greece, embrace the natural sweetness of fresh berries, and revel in the joy of a keto-friendly dessert bursting with Mediterranean delight.

Enjoy the silky smoothness, savor the vibrant berry sauce, and celebrate the enchanting flavors of Greece with this exquisite Keto Greek Yogurt Panna Cotta. Opa!

## Low-Carb Loukoumades (Greek Donuts)

Experience the delectable delight of Low-Carb Loukoumades, a keto-friendly twist on the beloved Greek donuts. These fluffy bite-sized treats are crispy on the outside, pillowy soft on the inside, and drizzled with a sugar-free syrup, making them an irresistible keto Greek dessert that will satisfy your cravings without breaking your low-carb commitment.

Ingredients:
For the Loukoumades:
- 1 cup almond flour
- 1/4 cup coconut flour
- 2 tablespoons granulated keto sweetener
- 1/2 teaspoon baking powder
- 1/4 teaspoon salt
- 1/2 teaspoon ground cinnamon
- Pinch of nutmeg (optional)
- 3 large eggs
- 1/4 cup unsweetened almond milk (or any preferred low-carb milk)
- 1/2 teaspoon vanilla extract
- Coconut oil or ghee, for frying

For the Sugar-Free Syrup:
- 1/4 cup water
- 1/4 cup granulated keto sweetener
- 1/2 teaspoon lemon juice
- 1/2 teaspoon rose water or orange blossom water (optional)
- Ground cinnamon, for sprinkling (optional)

Instructions:
For the Loukoumades:
1. In a mixing bowl, whisk together the almond flour, coconut flour, keto sweetener, baking powder, salt, ground cinnamon, and nutmeg (if using).
2. In a separate bowl, whisk the eggs, almond milk, and vanilla extract until well combined.
3. Gradually add the wet ingredients to the dry ingredients, stirring until a smooth batter forms.
4. Heat the coconut oil or ghee in a deep saucepan or pot to approximately 350°F (180°C).
5. Using a small cookie scoop or a spoon, drop small portions of the batter into the hot oil, being careful not to overcrowd the pot.
6. Fry the loukoumades for about 2-3 minutes, or until they turn golden brown and puffed up. Flip them occasionally for even cooking.
7. Using a slotted spoon or tongs, transfer the loukoumades to a plate lined with paper towels to absorb any excess oil.

For the Sugar-Free Syrup:
1. In a small saucepan, combine water, keto sweetener, lemon juice, and rose water or orange blossom water (if using).
2. Bring the mixture to a gentle boil over medium heat, stirring occasionally, until the sweetener has completely dissolved and the syrup has slightly thickened, about 3-4 minutes.

3. Remove the syrup from the heat and let it cool for a few minutes.

To Serve:
1. Drizzle the warm loukoumades with the sugar-free syrup, ensuring they are coated evenly.
2. Sprinkle with a dash of ground cinnamon, if desired, for an extra touch of aromatic flavor.
3. Serve immediately and savor the delightful indulgence of Low-Carb Loukoumades.

These Low-Carb Loukoumades capture the essence of the traditional Greek donuts, providing you with a guilt-free option that satisfies your sweet cravings while adhering to your low-carb lifestyle. The combination of almond flour, coconut flour, and natural keto sweetener creates a fluffy and flavorful base, and the sugar-free syrup adds just the right amount of sweetness to complete the experience.

As you take a bite into these delicate, crispy, and tender Greek donuts, relish the authentic flavors without compromising your dietary goals. Celebrate the joy of traditional Greek desserts, keto-style, and experience the bliss of indulging in Low-Carb Loukoumades. Opa!

## Keto Galaktoboureko (Custard Pie)

Savor the velvety smoothness of a Greek classic with a keto twist in this delightful Keto Galaktoboureko (Custard Pie). With layers of golden phyllo pastry and a luscious custard filling, each forkful of this low-carb dessert will transport you to the heart of Greece. Indulge in the richness and sweetness of this traditional treat while staying true to your ketogenic lifestyle.

Ingredients:
For the Phyllo Pastry:
- 6 sheets of keto-friendly phyllo dough (or homemade keto phyllo dough)

For the Custard Filling:
- 4 cups unsweetened almond milk
- 1/2 cup granulated keto sweetener
- 1/4 cup unsalted butter
- 1/2 cup almond flour
- 1/4 cup coconut flour
- 4 large eggs
- 1 teaspoon vanilla extract
- Zest of 1 lemon
- Ground cinnamon, for sprinkling

For the Syrup:
- 1/2 cup water
- 1/2 cup granulated keto sweetener
- 1 tablespoon lemon juice
- 1 cinnamon stick
- Rose water or orange blossom water, for flavoring (optional)

Instructions:
For the Phyllo Pastry:
1. Preheat the oven to 350°F (175°C).
2. Lightly grease a baking dish and place a sheet of phyllo pastry at the bottom. Brush it with melted butter.
3. Repeat the process, layering the remaining phyllo sheets one by one, brushing each with melted butter.
4. Trim any excess phyllo pastry hanging over the edges of the baking dish.

For the Custard Filling:
1. In a saucepan, heat the almond milk over medium heat until hot but not boiling. Remove from heat.
2. In a separate bowl, whisk together the keto sweetener, almond flour, coconut flour, eggs, vanilla extract, and lemon zest until well combined.
3. Slowly pour the hot almond milk into the egg mixture, whisking continuously to prevent curdling.
4. Return the custard mixture to the saucepan and cook over medium heat, stirring constantly, until it thickens to a custard-like consistency.

5. Pour the custard filling over the phyllo pastry layers in the baking dish, spreading it evenly.
6. Bake in the preheated oven for about 40-45 minutes, or until the top is golden brown and the custard is set.

For the Syrup:
1. In a small saucepan, combine the water, keto sweetener, lemon juice, cinnamon stick, and rose water or orange blossom water (if using).
2. Bring the syrup to a gentle simmer over medium heat and cook for about 5 minutes until slightly thickened.
3. Remove the cinnamon stick and set the syrup aside to cool.

To Serve:
1. Once the Galaktoboureko (Custard Pie) is baked and slightly cooled, pour the cooled syrup over the top, ensuring it is evenly distributed.
2. Let the pie cool completely before chilling in the refrigerator for a few hours or overnight to set.
3. Prior to serving, sprinkle the top of the pie with a generous dusting of ground cinnamon.
4. Cut into slices and enjoy the indulgent Keto Galaktoboureko (Custard Pie).

With its delicate layers of phyllo pastry and creamy custard filling, this Keto Galaktoboureko brings the joy of traditional Greek desserts to your low-carb table. Each bite reveals a harmonious blend of textures and flavors, crowned with the sweetness of the syrup and the warmth of cinnamon.

Celebrate the richness of Greek cuisine, embrace the beauty of traditional desserts, and satisfy your cravings with this divine Keto Galaktoboureko (Custard Pie). Relish in the magic of Greece, keto-style, and enjoy this delightful dessert while staying on track with your ketogenic journey. Opa!

# Cuisine Fusion (Greek and Other Cuisines)

Welcome to the exciting realm of cuisine fusion, where we embark on a culinary adventure that blends the rich flavors of Greek cuisine with elements from other culinary traditions. In this chapter, we will explore how the principles of the ketogenic diet intertwine with the diverse world of Greek and international cuisines, creating innovative and eclectic dishes that will expand your gastronomic horizons.

Food fusion has become a source of inspiration for chefs and home cooks alike, allowing us to explore new flavors, techniques, and ingredients while honoring the roots of each culinary tradition. By embracing the fusion of Greek cuisine with other global flavors, we can create harmonious and tantalizing dishes that offer a unique twist on familiar classics.

In this chapter, we will dive into the immense possibilities of cuisine fusion and discover how Greek cuisine can seamlessly integrate with other culinary heritages while still adhering to the principles of the ketogenic lifestyle. From Mediterranean Buddha bowls that combine the essence of Greece with the vibrant flavors of other Mediterranean countries, to Greek-inspired keto pizza that reimagines beloved Greek ingredients on a low-carb crust, we will embark on a journey that transcends borders and celebrates the beautiful tapestry of global cuisine.

By infusing Greek cuisine with elements from other culinary traditions, we can ignite our taste buds with new and exciting flavors, while also reaping the benefits of the ketogenic diet. We will explore how these fusion creations can provide balanced nutrition, delicious taste, and a sense of adventure in our everyday meals.

So, whether you're a seasoned keto warrior looking to inject variety into your meals or a culinary explorer seeking new ways to celebrate the flavors of Greece, this chapter will inspire and delight your senses. Get ready to venture into uncharted territory as we embark on a fusion feast that blends the best of Greek cuisine with elements from around the world.

Join me in embracing the fusion of old and new, tradition and innovation, as we explore the possibilities in this exciting chapter of Keto Greek. Let your taste buds traverse continents, and let the flavors of Greece blend harmoniously with other culinary traditions. Together, let's celebrate the beauty of diversity and revel in the delectable results of cuisine fusion. Opa!

## Mediterranean Keto Buddha Bowl

Indulge in a harmonious blend of Mediterranean flavors with this vibrant and nutritious Mediterranean Keto Buddha Bowl. In this recipe, we combine Greek-inspired ingredients with elements from other Mediterranean cuisines to create a wholesome and satisfying bowl that will transport you to the sunny shores of the Mediterranean.

Ingredients:

For the Bowl:
- 1 cup cauliflower rice
- 2 cups baby spinach
- 1/2 cup cherry tomatoes, halved
- 1/2 cup diced cucumber
- 1/4 cup sliced red onion
- 1/4 cup sliced Kalamata olives
- 2 tablespoons crumbled feta cheese
- Fresh parsley, for garnish

For the Lemon Tahini Dressing:
- 2 tablespoons tahini
- 2 tablespoons extra-virgin olive oil
- 1 tablespoon freshly squeezed lemon juice
- 1 clove garlic, minced
- Salt and pepper, to taste
- Water, as needed to achieve desired consistency

Instructions:

1. Prepare the lemon tahini dressing by whisking together tahini, olive oil, lemon juice, minced garlic, salt, and pepper in a small bowl. Gradually add water, a tablespoon at a time, until the dressing reaches your desired consistency. Set aside.

2. In a large bowl, assemble the Buddha bowl by layering cauliflower rice, baby spinach, cherry tomatoes, diced cucumber, sliced red onion, Kalamata olives, and crumbled feta cheese.

3. Drizzle the lemon tahini dressing over the bowl, allowing the flavors to meld together.

4. Garnish with fresh parsley for added freshness and color.

5. Toss the ingredients gently to combine or enjoy the bowl as a layered presentation.

This Mediterranean Keto Buddha Bowl showcases the vibrant colors and distinctive flavors of the Mediterranean region. The cauliflower rice provides a low-carb base, while the combination of baby spinach, cherry tomatoes, cucumber, red onion, and Kalamata olives adds a refreshing and invigorating element. The crumbled feta cheese brings a tangy and creamy note that ties all the ingredients together.

The lemon tahini dressing serves as the perfect finishing touch, adding a velvety richness and a hint of tanginess to complement the Mediterranean flavors. It brings together the essence of Greek cuisine with a nod to the broader Mediterranean culinary heritage, creating a cohesive and incredibly satisfying meal.

Whether you enjoy this Mediterranean Keto Buddha Bowl as a light lunch, a quick dinner, or a meal prep option, it's a delightful way to elevate your ketogenic eating experience. Allow the flavors of the Mediterranean to transport you to sun-drenched landscapes as you savor each bite of this colorful and nourishing bowl.

So, embrace the fusion of Mediterranean cuisines, celebrate the versatility of Greek-inspired ingredients, and revel in the healthy indulgence of this Mediterranean Keto Buddha Bowl. Enjoy the culinary voyage, and let the tantalizing flavors whisk you away on a journey of culinary discovery. Opa!

## Greek-inspired Keto Pizza

Experience the best of both worlds with this Greek-inspired Keto Pizza that combines the beloved flavors of Greek cuisine with the low-carb, high-fat principles of the ketogenic diet. In this recipe, we reimagine the classic pizza by incorporating Greek ingredients and Mediterranean flair, creating a delicious and guilt-free pizza experience.

Ingredients:

For the Crust:
- 1 1/2 cups shredded mozzarella cheese
- 3/4 cup almond flour
- 2 tablespoons cream cheese
- 1 large egg
- 1 teaspoon dried oregano
- 1/2 teaspoon garlic powder
- Salt and pepper, to taste

For the Toppings:
- 1/4 cup sugar-free tomato sauce or crushed tomatoes
- 1/2 cup diced cooked chicken or gyro meat (optional)
- 1/4 cup sliced Kalamata olives
- 1/4 cup sliced red onion
- 1/4 cup crumbled feta cheese
- Fresh oregano or basil leaves, for garnish (optional)

Instructions:

1. Preheat the oven to 425°F (220°C) and line a pizza stone or baking sheet with parchment paper.

2. In a microwave-safe bowl, combine the shredded mozzarella cheese and cream cheese. Microwave for 1-2 minutes, stirring every 30 seconds, until the cheese is melted and well combined.

3. Add the almond flour, egg, dried oregano, garlic powder, salt, and pepper to the melted cheese mixture. Stir until all the ingredients are thoroughly incorporated and form a dough-like consistency.

4. Transfer the dough onto the lined pizza stone or baking sheet. Flatten it into a circular shape, about 1/4 inch thick. If the dough sticks to your hands, lightly dampen them with water or oil.

5. Bake the crust in the preheated oven for approximately 10-12 minutes or until it is golden brown and crisp around the edges.

6. Once the crust is baked, remove it from the oven and let it cool for a few minutes.

7. Spread the sugar-free tomato sauce or crushed tomatoes evenly over the crust, leaving a small border around the edges.

8. Sprinkle the diced cooked chicken or gyro meat (if using) over the sauce, followed by the sliced Kalamata olives and red onion.

9. Crumble the feta cheese on top of the pizza, distributing it evenly.

10. Return the pizza to the oven and bake for an additional 7-10 minutes or until the cheese has melted and the toppings are heated through.

11. Once the pizza is cooked to your desired level of crispness, remove it from the oven and let it cool for a couple of minutes.

12. Garnish with fresh oregano or basil leaves, if desired.

This Greek-inspired Keto Pizza offers a delightful combination of flavors that will transport you to the streets of Athens or the beautiful islands of Greece. The crust, made from a blend of melted mozzarella cheese, almond flour, and seasonings, provides a satisfying base that perfectly complements the Greek-inspired toppings.

From the tanginess of the feta cheese to the briny Kalamata olives and the savory red onion, the toppings bring an authentic taste of Greece to this keto-friendly pizza. You can also customize your Greek-inspired Keto Pizza with additional toppings such as fresh tomatoes, bell peppers, or even tzatziki sauce for an extra burst of flavor.

Whether you're hosting a Greek-themed dinner party or simply craving a guilt-free pizza night, this Greek-inspired Keto Pizza will satisfy your taste buds while supporting your ketogenic lifestyle goals. Revel in the Mediterranean flavors and indulge in the joy of pizza without the carb overload.

So, embrace the fusion of Greek cuisine and the ketogenic diet, gather your favorite toppings, and satiate your pizza cravings with this Greek-inspired Keto Pizza. Eat, enjoy, and exclaim with delight, "Opa!"

## Keto Greek Nachos with Lamb

Experience a delightful fusion of Greek and Mexican flavors with these tantalizing Keto Greek Nachos with Lamb. In this recipe, we bring together the bold and vibrant elements of Greek cuisine with the beloved concept of nachos, creating a mouthwatering dish that will excite your tastebuds and transport you to a world of culinary fusion.

Ingredients:

For the Lamb:
- 1 pound ground lamb
- 1 tablespoon olive oil
- 1 small onion, finely chopped
- 2 cloves garlic, minced
- 1 teaspoon dried oregano
- 1/2 teaspoon ground cumin
- Salt and pepper, to taste

For the Nachos:
- 1 batch of homemade or store-bought keto tortilla chips
- 1 cup shredded mozzarella cheese
- 1/4 cup crumbled feta cheese
- 1/4 cup diced cucumber
- 1/4 cup diced tomatoes
- 2 tablespoons chopped Kalamata olives
- 2 tablespoons chopped fresh parsley
- Tzatziki sauce, for drizzling (optional)

Instructions:

1. In a skillet, heat the olive oil over medium heat. Add the chopped onion and minced garlic, sautéing until softened and fragrant.

2. Add the ground lamb to the skillet, breaking it up with a spoon. Cook until browned and cooked through.

3. Season the lamb with dried oregano, ground cumin, salt, and pepper. Mix well to ensure the flavors are evenly distributed. Remove from heat and set aside.

4. Preheat the oven to 350°F (175°C).

5. Arrange the keto tortilla chips in a single layer on a baking sheet or oven-safe dish.

6. Sprinkle the shredded mozzarella cheese over the tortilla chips, followed by the crumbled feta cheese.

7. Spread the cooked lamb evenly over the cheese-topped tortilla chips.

8. Top with diced cucumber, diced tomatoes, and chopped Kalamata olives.

9. Place the baking sheet or dish in the preheated oven and bake for approximately 8-10 minutes, or until the cheese is melted and bubbly.

10. Remove from the oven and garnish with chopped fresh parsley.

11. Drizzle with tzatziki sauce, if desired, for a creamy and tangy finish.

These Keto Greek Nachos with Lamb offer a delightful twist on the beloved Mexican nachos, infusing them with the bold flavors of Greek cuisine. The juicy and flavorful ground lamb, seasoned with aromatic spices, brings the essence of Greek cuisine to the forefront. The combination of shredded mozzarella and crumbled feta cheeses adds a luscious creaminess and a tangy note that perfectly complements the lamb.

Topped with fresh cucumbers, tomatoes, Kalamata olives, and a sprinkling of parsley, these nachos provide a refreshing and vibrant array of textures and flavors. You can customize the toppings further with additional Greek-inspired ingredients such as tzatziki sauce, diced red onion, or even a squeeze of lemon juice for an extra burst of brightness.

These Keto Greek Nachos with Lamb are a satisfying and indulgent dish that will delight your taste buds while adhering to your ketogenic lifestyle. Perfect for a casual gathering, game night, or even as a unique dinner option, these nachos offer a wonderful fusion of Greek and Mexican cuisines.

So, embrace the fusion of flavors, gather your ingredients, and prepare to savor the deliciousness of these Keto Greek Nachos with Lamb. Opa! Let the joy of culinary fusion transport you to a world of delightful flavors and happy taste buds.

## Greek-style Cauliflower Tabbouleh

Delight in a fresh and vibrant fusion of Greek and Middle Eastern flavors with this Keto Greek-style Cauliflower Tabbouleh. This unique twist on the traditional tabbouleh salad replaces the bulgur wheat with cauliflower, creating a low-carb and keto-friendly version that still bursts with the tantalizing flavors of Greece and the Middle East.

Ingredients:

- 1 medium cauliflower head, riced
- 1 cup finely chopped fresh parsley
- 1/4 cup finely chopped fresh mint leaves
- 1/2 cup diced cucumbers
- 1/2 cup diced tomatoes
- 1/4 cup finely chopped red onion
- 1/4 cup Kalamata olives, pitted and chopped
- Juice of 1 lemon
- 3 tablespoons extra-virgin olive oil
- Salt and pepper, to taste

Instructions:

1. Begin by preparing the cauliflower rice. Cut the cauliflower into florets, then place them in a food processor. Pulse until the cauliflower resembles rice-like grains. Set aside.

2. In a large mixing bowl, combine the cauliflower rice, finely chopped parsley, chopped mint leaves, diced cucumbers, diced tomatoes, chopped red onion, and chopped Kalamata olives.

3. In a separate small bowl, whisk together the lemon juice, extra-virgin olive oil, salt, and pepper to create the dressing.

4. Drizzle the dressing over the cauliflower mixture and toss gently to coat the ingredients evenly.

5. Let the Greek-style cauliflower tabbouleh sit for 10-15 minutes to allow the flavors to meld together.

6. Serve chilled or at room temperature, and enjoy the refreshing and vibrant flavors of this unique Greek-inspired tabbouleh.

This Greek-style Cauliflower Tabbouleh offers a lighter spin on the traditional tabbouleh salad while maintaining the essence of Greek and Middle Eastern flavors. The cauliflower rice serves as a nutritious and low-carb substitute for traditional bulgur wheat, making it suitable for those following a ketogenic lifestyle.

The combination of fresh parsley, mint, cucumbers, tomatoes, red onion, and Kalamata olives brings a burst of freshness to the dish. The zesty lemon juice and extra-virgin olive oil dressing tie all the ingredients together, infusing them with tangy and aromatic notes that perfectly complement the Greek-inspired theme.

Whether enjoyed as a refreshing side dish, a light lunch, or even as a main course, this Greek-style Cauliflower Tabbouleh offers a delightful fusion of flavors that will transport your taste buds to the sunny shores of Greece and the Middle East.

So, embrace this creative culinary fusion, savor the freshness of the ingredients, and enjoy the healthy and delicious experience of this Keto Greek-style Cauliflower Tabbouleh. Let the vibrant flavors transport you to a Mediterranean oasis, while still staying true to your ketogenic lifestyle. Opa!

## Special Occasions and Entertaining

In this chapter, we venture into the realm of special occasions and entertaining, where the flavors and culinary traditions of Greek cuisine take center stage. From festive gatherings to intimate celebrations, Greek cuisine has a rich heritage of bringing people together through delectable dishes and joyful feasts. In this section, we will explore how to adapt traditional Greek recipes for special occasions while maintaining the principles of the ketogenic lifestyle.

Special occasions call for extraordinary culinary experiences, and Greek cuisine has a remarkable repertoire of dishes that are perfect for such moments. Whether it's a birthday, a holiday celebration, or a gathering of friends and loved ones, the recipes in this chapter will help you create memorable events filled with the vibrancy and richness of Greek flavors.

We understand the importance of maintaining a ketogenic lifestyle, even during these special occasions. Therefore, each recipe in this chapter has been carefully crafted to ensure a low-carb, high-fat balance while staying true to the essence and authenticity of Greek cuisine. So, whether you're hosting a dinner party or attending a potluck, you can confidently serve these dishes, knowing they will impress and satisfy both guests and fellow keto enthusiasts.

From mouthwatering sliders inspired by moussaka to finger-licking shrimp skewers marinated in lemon and garlic, this chapter will guide you through a gastronomic adventure of Greek specialties adapted for ketogenic indulgence. You will also find delightful appetizers like low-carb spanakopita bites and Greek-style mini meatballs, all designed to dazzle your guests with flavors reminiscent of the Mediterranean.

As you explore the recipes in this chapter, feel free to adapt and personalize them to suit your preferences or dietary needs. The versatility of Greek cuisine allows for creativity and experimentation, so don't be afraid to put your own twist on these exceptional dishes.

So, whether you're planning a grand celebration or simply want to elevate your intimate gathering, allow the ketogenic Greek recipes in this chapter to be your culinary companions. Through flavors, aromas, and the conviviality of Greek traditions, create special memories that will linger in the hearts and palates of those you share them with.

Get ready to elevate your special occasions and entertain with the captivating allure of Greek cuisine, masterfully adapted for the ketogenic lifestyle. Let the festivities begin, and may this chapter inspire you to create unforgettable moments brimming with the flavors of Greece. Yasas and joyful celebrations await!

## Keto Moussaka Sliders

Add a touch of Greek elegance and indulgence to your special occasions with these mouthwatering Keto Moussaka Sliders. Inspired by the beloved Greek dish, these sliders bring together the rich flavors of ground meat, eggplant, and creamy béchamel sauce in a low-carb, bite-sized form that will leave your guests craving for more.

Ingredients:
For the sliders:
- 1 pound ground beef or lamb
- 1 small onion, finely chopped
- 2 cloves garlic, minced
- 1 teaspoon dried oregano
- 1/2 teaspoon ground cinnamon
- Salt and pepper, to taste
- Olive oil, for cooking
- Sliced eggplant, grilled or roasted

For the béchamel sauce:
- 2 tablespoons unsalted butter
- 2 tablespoons almond flour
- 1 cup unsweetened almond milk (or another non-dairy milk)
- 1/4 cup grated Parmesan cheese
- Pinch of nutmeg
- Salt and white pepper, to taste

For serving:
- Slider buns (keto-friendly or lettuce wraps for a low-carb option)
- Sliced tomatoes
- Fresh parsley, for garnish

Instructions:
1. In a mixing bowl, combine the ground beef or lamb, chopped onion, minced garlic, dried oregano, ground cinnamon, salt, and pepper. Mix well to incorporate all the ingredients evenly.
2. Divide the meat mixture into small patties, sized to fit the slider buns.
3. Heat a drizzle of olive oil in a skillet over medium-high heat. Cook the patties for 3-4 minutes on each side, or until cooked to your desired level of doneness.
4. In a separate saucepan, melt the butter over medium heat. Add the almond flour and whisk until well combined.
5. Gradually pour the almond milk into the saucepan, whisking continuously to avoid any lumps.
6. Stir in the grated Parmesan cheese, nutmeg, salt, and white pepper. Continue whisking until the sauce thickens and reaches a creamy consistency.
7. Remove the slider patties from the skillet and set them aside. In the same skillet, add the sliced eggplant and cook until softened and lightly browned.
8. Assemble the sliders: Place a slider patty on the bottom half of each bun or lettuce wrap. Top with a slice of cooked eggplant and drizzle with the béchamel sauce.

9. Garnish with sliced tomatoes and fresh parsley for added freshness and visual appeal.
10. Serve these delectable Keto Moussaka Sliders to your guests and watch as they savor the extraordinary flavors of Greek cuisine, beautifully adapted for the ketogenic lifestyle.

With their aromatic spices and creamy béchamel sauce, these sliders are a tantalizing combination of Greek flavors in a portable and convenient form. The grilled or roasted eggplant adds a delightful smokiness and enhances the texture, while the rich béchamel sauce brings a touch of sophistication to the sliders.

Whether you're hosting a dinner party, celebrating a special occasion, or simply want to wow your family and friends, these Keto Moussaka Sliders are a perfect choice. Each bite will transport your guests to the idyllic streets of Greece, where the aroma of Mediterranean herbs and spices fills the air.

So, prepare to impress and delight with these elegant and flavorsome sliders. Let the spirit of the Greek cuisine shine through as you celebrate in style, showcasing the versatility of Greek flavors adapted for the ketogenic lifestyle. Kali orexi and enjoy these Keto Moussaka Sliders with your loved ones!

## Lemon and Garlic Shrimp Skewers

Take your special occasions to the next level with the vibrant flavors of these delectable Lemon and Garlic Shrimp Skewers. Inspired by the coastal delights of Greece, these keto-friendly skewers will transport you and your guests to the shores of the Mediterranean, where the aroma of grilled seafood dances in the air.

Ingredients:
- 1 pound large shrimp, peeled and deveined
- 3 cloves garlic, minced
- Zest and juice of 1 lemon
- 2 tablespoons olive oil
- 1 tablespoon chopped fresh parsley
- 1/2 teaspoon dried oregano
- Salt and pepper, to taste
- Skewers (metal or soaked wooden skewers)

Instructions:
1. In a mixing bowl, combine the minced garlic, lemon zest, lemon juice, olive oil, chopped parsley, dried oregano, salt, and pepper. Stir well to create a marinade.
2. Add the peeled and deveined shrimp to the marinade and toss to coat each shrimp thoroughly. Let the shrimp marinate for at least 20 minutes to allow the flavors to meld together.
3. Preheat a grill or grill pan over medium-high heat.
4. Skewer the marinated shrimp, threading them onto the skewers.
5. Place the skewers on the preheated grill and cook for 2-3 minutes on each side, or until the shrimp turn pink and opaque.
6. Remove the skewers from the grill and garnish with additional lemon zest and fresh parsley, if desired.
7. Serve these tantalizing Lemon and Garlic Shrimp Skewers as an impressive appetizer or main dish for your special occasion, and watch your guests revel in the flavors of Greece.

These Lemon and Garlic Shrimp Skewers encapsulate the freshness and vibrancy of Greek coastal cuisine. The zesty lemon and pungent garlic create a delightful marinade that enhances the natural sweetness of the shrimp, resulting in a perfectly balanced dish.

Whether served as an appetizer or main course, these skewers will impress both seafood lovers and fans of Greek cuisine. The light and tangy flavors will transport your taste buds to the sun-soaked beaches of Greece, where the simplicity of the ingredients shines through.

So, fire up the grill, let the enticing aromas fill the air, and bask in the joy of sharing these Lemon and Garlic Shrimp Skewers with your loved ones. Enjoy the camaraderie, the celebration, and the flavors of the Mediterranean as you create unforgettable memories on your special occasions. Yasas and bon appétit!

## Low-Carb Spanakopita Bites

Impress your guests with these irresistible Low-Carb Spanakopita Bites, a delightful twist on the classic Greek dish. Bursting with the flavors of spinach, feta cheese, and fragrant herbs, these bite-sized appetizers bring the essence of Greece to your special occasion while adhering to the principles of a low-carb lifestyle.

Ingredients:
- 1 package of phyllo dough sheets (keto-friendly or homemade low-carb phyllo dough, if preferred)
- 2 cups fresh spinach, finely chopped
- 1/2 cup crumbled feta cheese
- 1/4 cup chopped fresh dill
- 2 green onions, finely chopped
- 2 tablespoons olive oil
- Salt and pepper, to taste
- Melted butter or olive oil for brushing

Instructions:
1. Preheat the oven to the temperature indicated on the phyllo dough package.
2. In a mixing bowl, combine the chopped spinach, crumbled feta cheese, chopped fresh dill, green onions, olive oil, salt, and pepper. Mix well until all the ingredients are evenly incorporated.
3. Lay out one phyllo dough sheet and brush it lightly with melted butter or olive oil. Place another sheet on top and repeat the process until you have about 4-6 layers.
4. Cut the layered phyllo dough into rectangles or squares, depending on your desired bite size.
5. Spoon a small amount of the spinach and cheese mixture onto each cut piece of phyllo dough.
6. Gently fold the phyllo dough around the filling, creating a small package or triangle shape.
7. Place the spanakopita bites on a baking sheet lined with parchment paper.
8. Brush the tops of the bites with melted butter or olive oil.
9. Bake in the preheated oven for the time indicated on the phyllo dough package, or until the bites are golden brown and crispy.
10. Remove from the oven and let the spanakopita bites cool slightly before serving.

These Low-Carb Spanakopita Bites offer a delightful combination of flaky phyllo dough, savory spinach, and tangy feta cheese. Each bite-sized morsel presents a burst of Greek flavors that will captivate your guests and transport them to the tavernas of Greece.

Feel free to personalize these bites by adjusting the size, shape, or filling to suit your preferences. You can experiment with different herbs, such as mint or parsley, or even add a touch of lemon zest for an extra zing. The versatility of spanakopita allows for endless creativity while maintaining the essence of this beloved Greek dish.

Prepare to impress your guests with these delectable Low-Carb Spanakopita Bites. Embrace the joy of entertaining and savor the flavors of Greece in a way that aligns with your low-carb lifestyle. Each bite is an invitation to embark on a culinary journey and celebrate the beauty of Greek cuisine with those you hold dear. Efcharistó! Enjoy!

## Greek-style Mini Meatballs with Tzatziki Sauce

Elevate your special occasions with the exquisite flavors of Greek-style Mini Meatballs served with tangy Tzatziki Sauce. These bite-sized gems will dazzle your guests and bring the essence of Greek cuisine to your table, all while staying true to the principles of a ketogenic lifestyle.

Ingredients:
For the mini meatballs:
- 1 pound ground beef or lamb
- 1 small onion, finely diced
- 2 cloves garlic, minced
- 1/4 cup almond flour
- 2 tablespoons chopped fresh parsley
- 1 tablespoon chopped fresh mint
- 1 teaspoon dried oregano
- 1/2 teaspoon ground cumin
- Salt and pepper, to taste
- Olive oil, for cooking

For the tzatziki sauce:
- 1 cup Greek yogurt
- 1/2 cucumber, grated and squeezed to remove excess moisture
- 1 clove garlic, minced
- 1 tablespoon lemon juice
- 1 tablespoon chopped fresh dill
- Salt and pepper, to taste

Instructions:
For the mini meatballs:
1. Preheat the oven to 375°F (190°C) and line a baking sheet with parchment paper.
2. In a mixing bowl, combine the ground beef or lamb, diced onion, minced garlic, almond flour, chopped parsley, chopped mint, dried oregano, ground cumin, salt, and pepper. Mix well to ensure all the ingredients are evenly incorporated.
3. Roll the mixture into bite-sized meatballs, about 1 inch in diameter.
4. Heat a drizzle of olive oil in a skillet over medium-high heat. Cook the meatballs in batches until browned on all sides, then transfer them to the prepared baking sheet.
5. Place the meatballs in the preheated oven and bake for 10-12 minutes, or until cooked through.
6. Remove from the oven and let the mini meatballs cool slightly before serving.

For the tzatziki sauce:
1. In a bowl, combine the Greek yogurt, grated cucumber, minced garlic, lemon juice, chopped dill, salt, and pepper. Stir well to combine.
2. Taste and adjust the seasoning as needed, adding more lemon juice, salt or pepper to suit your preference.
3. Transfer the tzatziki sauce to a serving bowl and refrigerate for at least 30 minutes to allow the flavors to meld together.

To serve:
1. Arrange the Greek-style Mini Meatballs on a platter or skewers for an elegant presentation.
2. Serve alongside the chilled Tzatziki Sauce for dipping.

These Greek-style Mini Meatballs with Tzatziki Sauce will dazzle your taste buds with the bold flavors of the Mediterranean. The combination of aromatic herbs, spices, and tender meat will transport your guests to the idyllic tavernas of Greece.

Impress your friends and loved ones with these bite-sized delights that are both delicious and keto-friendly. The fresh and tangy Tzatziki Sauce perfectly complements the savory meatballs, creating a symphony of flavors that will leave your guests craving for more.

So, embrace the warmth and conviviality of Greek cuisine with these exquisite Mini Meatballs. Celebrate special moments with your loved ones, creating memories filled with the flavors of Greece and the joy of a ketogenic lifestyle. Kali orexi and enjoy this delicious Greek-inspired dish!

## Outro: Embracing the Ketogenic Lifestyle

Congratulations! You have reached the end of this culinary journey through the world of keto Greek cooking. We hope that this book has not only tantalized your taste buds but also provided you with the inspiration and knowledge to embrace the ketogenic lifestyle while enjoying the rich flavors of Greek cuisine.

As you have discovered throughout these chapters, the ketogenic diet offers numerous benefits beyond weight loss. By reducing carbohydrate intake and increasing healthy fats, you can experience improved energy levels, mental clarity, and overall well-being. The combination of the ketogenic principles with the vibrant flavors of Greek cooking has allowed for the creation of satisfying and nourishing meals that adhere to your dietary goals.

Throughout this book, we explored a variety of Greek breakfasts, appetizers, soups and salads, mains and sides, desserts, fusion dishes, and special occasion recipes, all tailored to the ketogenic lifestyle. We revisited traditional Greek ingredients, such as feta cheese, olive oil, and fresh herbs, and transformed them into keto-friendly creations bursting with Mediterranean flavors.

But this journey does not have to end here. Embracing the ketogenic lifestyle means integrating it into your everyday routine and adapting it to your own unique preferences and needs. Here are some tips and resources to help you continue on your keto Greek culinary adventure:

1. Personalize Your Keto Greek Culinary Journey: Experiment with different flavor combinations, spices, and herbs to create your own signature keto Greek dishes. Don't be afraid to get creative and adapt traditional Greek recipes to meet your taste preferences and dietary goals.

2. Explore Greek Ingredients and Local Markets: Greek cuisine is celebrated for its use of fresh and seasonal ingredients. Visit local farmers' markets or specialty stores to discover an array of Greek ingredients that can add authenticity and depth to your keto Greek creations.

3. Stay Informed: Keep up to date with research, books, and online resources that provide valuable insights into the ketogenic diet. Understand the science behind it, and continue learning about the health benefits and potential adaptations to enhance your well-being.

4. Seek Community Support: Connect with like-minded individuals who are also following the ketogenic lifestyle. Join online forums or local keto support groups to share recipes, tips, and experiences. Building a supportive community can help you stay motivated and inspired on your journey.

5. Listen to Your Body: Pay attention to how your body responds to different foods and adjust your keto Greek meals accordingly. Everyone's dietary needs and tolerances are unique, so be mindful of how specific ingredients or combinations make you feel.

6. Adapt Traditional Greek Celebrations: As you continue your keto Greek journey, consider adapting traditional Greek celebrations and feasts to align with your dietary goals. Explore ways to recreate festive dishes by substituting high-carb ingredients with keto-friendly alternatives, ensuring that you still indulge in the joyous spirit of Greek traditions.

Remember, the ketogenic lifestyle is not just a diet but a holistic approach to wellness. It's about nourishing your body, enjoying meals that fuel you, and embracing the culinary heritage of Greece in a way that aligns with your health goals.

We sincerely hope that this book has ignited your passion for Greek cuisine and inspired you to embark on a lifetime of delicious, keto-friendly meals. By combining the best of Greek flavors with the principles of the ketogenic diet, you have the power to transform your relationship with food, enhance your well-being, and savor the joys of life to the fullest.

So, gather your apron, stock up your pantry with Greek ingredients, and continue your keto Greek journey with enthusiasm and delight. May your meals be nourishing, your taste buds satisfied, and your spirit lifted by the harmonious blend of Greek and ketogenic flavors.

Thank you for joining us on this delectable adventure. Wishing you success, health, and many memorable keto Greek meals ahead. Yasas and Kali Orexi! Cheers and enjoy your meal!

Printed in Great Britain
by Amazon